Casa Juanita, entrance. 80 Middle Road.

Lost
in
Wonderland

Cover photo: Venetian staircase, Villa des Cygnes.

Back Cover photo: Ellen Glendinning Frazer and Joel Harriman, Coconuts Party, 1927. *(Lucius Ordway Fraser Collection)*

LOST IN WONDERLAND

Reflections on Palm Beach

Augustus Mayhew

For my mother Lucille Sanderson Mayhew
for a lifetime of
help, encouragement and inspiration

Published by Palm Beach Editorial Services
3800 Merrill Avenue, West Palm Beach, FL 33405
United States of America

ISBN 978-0-9831530-2-3
Library of Congress Control Number 2012949611

Layout by DidotGraphicDesign.com

Copyright© 2012 Augustus Mayhew
All rights reserved, which includes the right to reproduce this book or portions thereof in any form whatsoever except as provided by the U.S. Copyright law.

Printed in the United States of America

CONTENTS

Introduction
Acknowledgments

I SKETCHES

Prelude to Palm Beach 15
Oil Swells – The Standard Oil Crowd in Palm Beach 27
Envisioning Palm Beach 43
Preserving the Status Quo – 1930s Palm Beach 51
Royal Palm Beach 61
Mr. Palm Beach – Charles Munn & Claude Dimick Reese 71

II SOCIAL SETS

Social History – Family, Faith & Club 81
Jewish Society in Old Palm Beach 103
Women of Worth 123
High Rollers – Gambling on Palm Beach 139
The Oasis Club 145
The Art Colony – Easels and Galleries 153

III SCENES

Great Gardens 167
Fish Tales 183
Showplace for Shops 189
Reel Life in Old Palm Beach 205
Palm Beach Modern 215
Everglades Island 233
Palm Beach Regency 243
Is it a Mizner? 253
Unforgettable Palm Beach 257

Introduction

"You used to be much more...muchier. You've lost your muchness."
- Alice in Wonderland, Lewis Carroll.

Bookstore shelves are lined with volumes about Palm Beach, as much a setting for a fictional roman á clef as the subject for an architect's pictorial. No matter your preference for the mirror or mirage, your perspective shaded by the mythical, make-believe or matter-of-fact, Palm Beach's past remains as elusive to grasp as its present proves enigmatic to explore.

On February 8, 1901 the *Palm Beach Daily News* observed, "Within the next ten days, there will be more wealth represented on Palm Beach than anywhere else on the continent. The Rockefellers, Vanderbilts, Goulds, and Astors are scheduled to arrive. They are not alone, as a large number of millionaires are coming each day." Ever since Henry Flagler transformed what was described then as "a narrow peninsula covered with cocoanut palms" into an international resort destination, Palm Beach has been an incomparable showcase for displaying illusions of grandeur. From its inception, Palm Beach was described as "the upper world of respectability, wealth, leisure, beauty, and culture." Hotel ballrooms, Mizner loggias, South Ocean Boulevard facades, and Worth Avenue shops set the stage for the rest of the world to catch a glimpse of the seasonal summit's social arbiters who were cast as international news figures.

(Left): Playa Riente, Great Hall. *(Historical Society of Palm Beach County.)*

More than a century later, millionaires now billionaires, moguls, magnates, and tycoons continue gravitating to the island's coveted houses with sky-high hedges and guarded walls. However much it may still be at the top-of-the-world, Palm Beach's unique sense of place has diminished.

Having become one of many affluent residential enclaves, Palm Beach has developed a common form of locational vertigo, having lost much of its colorful character and many of the acceptable eccentricities that once defined it. One after another, great houses were demolished; estates were subdivided. Midtown's public attractions and accommodations were displaced by condominiums. Private clubs prohibited publicizing events; members were restricted from any public mention of club activities. Profits outweighed ambience allowing bungalows and cottages to be supplanted by townhouses. The welcome mat for out-of-towners was taken up; commercial venues became exclusively town-serving.

Without the magic of the people and the places that put it on the map, in today's Palm Beach it is easy to become lost in wonderland.

Acknowledgments

Lost in Wonderland is a collection of articles originally published in the *Palm Beach Daily News* and *The New York Social Diary*. Rather than an epic history of Palm Beach, these essays are intended as personal observations and impressions about Palm Beach life.

I am grateful to Joyce Reingold, editor and publisher of the *Palm Beach Daily News,* and David Patrick Columbia/Jeff Hirsch at *The New York Social Diary*.

The photographs are from my own collection while the historic photographs are credited. Identifications and attributions were the best that I could research and any corrections and omissions will be made in the next edition. I am indebted to Debi Murray, chief curator and archives at the Historical Society of Palm Beach County, for her careful scrutiny of the text. Additionally, I appreciate the efforts of editor John Nelander.

Special thanks to the late Donald Curl for always sharing his scholarship and insights.

Playa Riente, Tile plaque.

# I. Sketches

Prelude to Palm Beach

Palm Beach has reigned among the world's top-tier social domains for so many years that the well-heeled might have forgotten there was ever anywhere else except this exclusive island refuge.

Nonetheless, a decade before Palm Beach became the rendezvous for private railroad cars and black-tie balls, the smart set converged at its Gilded Age predecessors — the Jekyll Island Club and St. Augustine's Hotel Ponce de Leon. Much of the allure of these forerunners has since faded. The offshore Jekyll Island Club is now a public hotel within a historic district and state park while the Hotel Ponce de Leon is a private liberal arts college. Palm Beach prevails as the ultimate destination to indulge the wealth of pleasures that visitors might not want to be seen treating themselves to at home.

After the Civil War, wealthy Northerners who were not sailing down the Nile River, taking the cure at Marienbad, or wagering at Monte Carlo's casino, headed south for the winter. Long Island's North Shore horse set could be found fox hunting at Aiken and turning the South Georgia-North Florida Red Hills into the "Quail Capital of the World." Cotton plantations became private hunting preserves. By 1885, Thomasville's Mitchell House and Piney Woods Hotel, both designed by New York architect J. A. Wood, accommodated Social Register swells in search of bird shoots and field lunches.

(Left) Top: Looking north across the croquet court from William Rockefeller's Indian Mound Cottage, a panoramic view of the Jekyll Island Cub exhibits the hotel's multi-generational design history, from the Victorian era's Queen Anne fortress-like turret to the early-20th-century attached multi-story apartments.

(Left) Bottom: The Hotel Ponce de Leon was considered the most modern luxurious resort in the world when oil baron turned hotelier Henry Flagler welcomed the first guests in January 1888.

During this same time, Thomas Carnegie purchased land north of the fever zone on Cumberland Island along the Georgia coast, eventually owning ninety percent of the island. Immediately north of Carnegie's private kingdom, fifty-three members of New York's Union Club and their friends acquired the five thousand seven-hundred acre Jekyll Island. In January 1888, they opened what became known as the world's richest, most exclusive and most inaccessible enclave. Shortly thereafter, Standard Oil tycoon Henry Flagler opened the resplendent Hotel Ponce de Leon in the heart of St. Augustine, the "Ancient City."

The Jekyll Island Club

Built during the height of the Gilded Age's popular private club era, The Jekyll Island Club's founders were said to account for as much as one-fifth of the country's wealth. John Eugene DuBignon and his brother-in-law, Newton Finney sold the island for $125,000 as a huntsman's paradise to this clique, who turned it into a hunting and recreational club. Their members had been selected from among New York's Union Club, the family and friends of William K. Vanderbilt, Pierre Lorillard, J. P. Morgan, Joseph Pulitzer, Marshall Field and William Rockefeller. With his new fortune, Mr. DuBignon moved off the island; his existing family's cottage became the club superintendent's house.

The club hired Charles A. Alexander, a Chicago architect, and William Horace Shaler, a landscape architect, to design their private retreat. Ground was broken in mid-August 1886 and the club officially opened in January 1888. Becoming a club member was never easy; new members were either family members or close business associates. Never intended as an exclusive male preserve, the club welcomed its first woman member in 1893. By the 1930s more than twenty-five percent of the members were women. The Club operated from January to April from 1888 to 1942.

The club's first building expansion was in 1901 when the multi-story southeast wing was added. It featured eight members' apartments on the first two floors. Above them, the floor was reserved for guest rooms. Staff quarters were assigned to the fourth floor.

(Right) Top Left: Tuxedo Park denizen Pierre Lorillard arrived at Jekyll Island with his dogs and horses ready for the hunt. The Lorillard yacht towed an auxiliary two-story boat equipped with stables and kennels.

(Right) Top Right: The hotel's lobby has retained much of the club's original atmosphere.

(Right) Bottom: At night, the hotel takes on a timeless aura. Designated a National Historic Landmark in 1978, the hotel's quiet ambience is enhanced by banning automobiles within the historic district.

Jekyll Island's Cottage Colony

From 1888 to 1928, club members built fourteen cottages to the north and south of the main clubhouse along the river and Old Plantation Road. They were designed in step with the club's unwritten aesthetic rule, simplicity. The early buildings were Victorian-inspired, Queen Anne, Beaux Arts and Shingle styles. Later, cottages were embellished with Italian Renaissance and Spanish styles. The architects were the nation's best known designers. They included David Adler, Charles Alling Gifford, John Russell Pope, and Carrère and Hastings. For the most part, their work remains nearly intact, forming a like-minded historic district surrounding the original hotel.

In 1896, the Sans Souci, a complex of six apartments, was built for club members. Among them was William Rockefeller, who also owned a cottage, and J. P. Morgan, who served as club president. Designed by Charles Alling Gifford across from the club's south lawn, the distinctive compound became known as the "House of Power."

In 1924, the *Architectural Record* described Crane Cottage as "the most expensive and elegant winter home ever built at Jekyll." Built in 1916 for Richard Teller Crane, Jr., the house was designed by Chicago architects David Adler and Henry C. Dangler.

At the far north end of the club's property, Villa Ospo was built for Walter Jennings of New York, club president from 1927 to 1933. Designed in a Spanish-Italian eclectic style in 1927 by John Russell Pope, "Villa Ospo," was named for Jekyll Island's earliest Indian settlers.

Cherokee Cottage was built in the Italian Renaissance style for Dr. and Mrs. G. F. Shrady of New York. Local historians believe it was designed by Carrere and Hastings, who during the same period designed the nearby Goodyear Cottage. Sited facing the river and next to Indian Mound, the Goodyear Cottage was built in 1906 for Frank Goodyear, a Buffalo, New York industrialist. The Jekyll Island Arts Association is now housed in the building.

(Left) Top: Sans Souci, known as the "House of Power" because of its wealthy residents, was designed by Charles Alling Gifford and built as a six-unit apartment complex in 1896.

(Left) Bottom: Designed by Carrere and Hastings, the Goodyear Cottage was built for industrialist Frank Goodyear. The Jekyll Island Arts Association is now housed in the building.

Directly across the south lawn from the main club house's distinctive turret, Indian Mound Cottage was first commissioned by Gordon McKay in 1892 before it was sold to William Rockefeller, who expanded the house into a twenty-five-room mansion. When the State of Georgia took over Jekyll Island in 1947, Indian Mound Cottage was the first to be renovated.

The State of Georgia turned Jekyll Island into a state park. Four years later, a causeway to the island was completed, allowing more year-round visitors. The state leased the facility to a hotel operator from the mid-1950s until the 1970s. It reopened in its present pristine condition in 1986.

When the Jekyll Island Club opened, Henry Flagler was already transitioning from the oil industry to the resort business, hastening to open his Hotel Ponce de Leon for its first guests.

The Hotel Ponce de Leon, St. Augustine

The *New York Evening Post* hailed the Hotel Ponce de Leon in 1888 as "finest piece of hotel architecture in this country." It still seems hard to believe that St. Augustine, now for the most part a weekend tourist town, was ever regarded as the "Winter Newport." But Henry Flagler's flagship four hundred and fifty-room Spanish Renaissance palatial resort was Florida's first luxury hotel where presidents, royalty and Social Register families checked in for a season of memorable pleasures.

Construction began in 1885. Three years later its fledgling architects, John Carrere and Thomas Hastings, were credited with revolutionizing hotel construction and design, having formulated a resort from a purely artistic point of view. Carrere and Hastings associate architect Bernard Maybeck supervised the hotel's construction and interior work. Built for $2.5 million with coquina concrete walls, salmon bricks and terracotta detailing, Flagler hired Louis C. Tiffany, then known as a painter, to oversee the interiors and design the stained glass windows. The oval-shaped multi-story dining room, fitted with Tiffany glass clerestory windows, featured a musician's gallery.

VirgilioTojetti painted the ceilings in the dining room and the grand parlor ceiling. Decorative artist George Maynard adorned the walls with murals and frescoes. The New York interior design firm Pottier and Stymus supplied the furnishings.

(Right): Hotel Ponce de Leon. The 150-foot square courtyard features a frog-and-turtle fountain with a geometric mosaic centerpiece shaped like a sword.

Designed with an ornamental non-structural cupola, the lobby's four-story rotunda was the crossing point between the hotel's private and public spaces. While the hotel was powered by electricity furnished by Thomas Edison, initially the rotunda was lit by gas and the beacon shone through a glass panel in the cupola. The lobby's lion's head electric lights were added in 1893. Set amidst the four stages of Spanish exploration, Maynard's female figures for the rotunda were painted and gilded representing the four elements crowned with a decorative gold-and-white dome in the Louis XVI style.

As significant as Jekyll Island and St. Augustine were in the making of Palm Beach, the Vanderbilt family's role in stimulating Henry Flagler's interest in Lake Worth should not be overlooked. In 1893, the same year Flagler acquired the lakefront property for the Royal Poinciana Hotel, a consortium led by Cornelius Vanderbilt acquired the large expanse of property at the north end of Lake Worth with "extensive game and fishing preserves."

Called the Juno Beach Development Company, according to press reports of the day, Vanderbilt and his partners, his son William K. Vanderbilt, Chauncey Depew, president of the New York Central Railroad, and Cornelius Vanderbilt Barton, had planned to build "a clubhouse and hotel by year's end."

C. V. Barton was named for his great-uncle, Commodore Cornelius Vanderbilt. Vanderbilt's sister had married Samuel Barton, a boyhood friend of the Commodore's. Barton's father, also named Samuel Barton, became one of the Vanderbilt family's trusted business advisors and for three generations, its principal broker. By 1886, C. V. Barton and his wife, the former Jessie Cluett, were already spending the winter on the east side of Lake Worth. Three years later, the Bartons were among the founding members of The Episcopal Church of Bethesda-by-the-Sea, known as one of the earliest houses of worship in Dade County.

For all of Palm Beach's luxuries and privileges, its exclusiveness, larger-than-life personalities, and grand houses, it has lost the sense of place that is still expressed among the ensemble of buildings that make up the Jekyll Island Club's and St. Augustine's historic district. Nonetheless, because

(Right) Top: The hotel lobby's four-story rotunda was designed with an ornamental non-structural cupola. The hotel was powered by electricity installed by Thomas Edison. After Henry Flagler died in Palm Beach, he was brought to St. Augustine where he lay in state in the hotel's rotunda beneath the cupola.

(Right) Bottom: The lobby-parlor was finished with elaborate ceiling plasterwork composed of interwoven medallions.

the popularity of Jekyll Island and the Hotel Ponce de Leon was short-lived, they have retained their defining architectural character, whereas much of Palm Beach's original charm has eroded, reduced to postcard memories of the past. The renowned Royal Poinciana Hotel was supplanted with a shopping center and condominium. Magnificent ocean-to-lake estates were carved up into subdivisions. For the most part, Royal Palm Way is now lined with unexceptional office buildings. And, perhaps most historically estranged, the town's oceanfront and lakefront are cluttered with multi-story condominiums.

But, while Palm Beach opted to do away with significant elements of its unique history, the Jekyll Island Club remains virtually untouched from when Union Club members first arrived on the island. And, thanks to Henry Flagler's selection of craftsmen, the Ponce de Leon's skillful artistry remains unrivaled even by today's Palm Beach standards. And even though Palm Beach may harbor almost all the money in the world, there is hardly a building comparable to the consummate aesthetic that endures at the Jekyll Island Club and the former Hotel Ponce de Leon.

(Left) Top Left: On the lobby ceiling, muralist George Maynard depicted an artistic history of Spanish exploration. Maynard's female figures were painted and gilded, representing the four stages of Spanish exploration, and crowned with a decorative gold-and-white dome in the Louis XVI style.

(Left) Top Right: The lobby's eight carved-oak caryatids were molded around hidden iron-rods. These unique structural columns were designed by architect Thomas Hastings who said the figures were inspired by the movement of Spanish dancers

(Left) Bottom: Henry Flagler was Carrere and Hastings' first major client; the Hotel Ponce de Leon, the firm's first major commission.

Oil Swells –
The Standard Oil crowd in Palm Beach

"Money-mad, money-mad! Sane in every other way, but money-mad."
- Senator Marcus A. Hanna's characterization of John D. Rockefeller. *The History of Standard Oil*, by Ida Minerva Tarbell.

As much today as it was a century ago, Palm Beach is a palm-shaded offshore refuge where reclusive bluebloods, corporate tycoons, and social aspirants retreat from the harsh light of the mainland's more accountable and less luxuriant ambience. The island's secret private clubs are as impregnable to outsiders as they were when the Old Guard cliques created them. And there was no more eminent or scrutinized Gilded Age social set within Henry Flagler's Florida resort empire than Standard Oil Company's trustees and their descendants.

By 1907, four years before the court-ordered Standard Oil trust breakup, the company's largest shareholders included: John D. Rockefeller, Daniel M. Harkness, Henry Flagler's half-brother, the Charles Pratt estate, Oliver Payne, Henry M. Flagler, Henry H. Rogers, the Jabez Bostwick estate, William Rockefeller, Henry M. Tilford, John D. Archbold, and William G. Warden. Most of these principals and their descendants found their way to Palm Beach.

(Left): Jean Flagler Matthews led the campaign to restore Whitehall, the Palm Beach mansion built by her grandfather and designed by Carrere and Hastings. "She was fun and vivacious," recalled Jim Ponce. "While it seemed everyone else was demolishing the big houses, amazingly, Jean stepped up and saved Whitehall". *(Palm Beach Daily News)*

The Standard crowd

During the winter of 1888, as private Pullman rail cars pulled out of New York heading to St. Augustine for the opening of Henry Flagler's Hotel Ponce de Leon, Albany's state legislators were launching their investigation into the Standard Oil Trust that more than two decades later would result in the Supreme Court's directive breaking up and reforming the company.

Despite pesky court subpoenas and annoying congressional hearings, the Standard Oil cartel's most prominent trustees escaped the glare of headlines and indictments sheltered within several social Gibraltars. Rather than being probed and questioned about the inner sanctum of the world's most powerful syndicate or denounced muckrakers, Euclid Avenue monopolists and Fifth Avenue

moguls engaged in quail hunts and golf games at their Thomasville plantations, Jekyll Island preserve, or in St. Augustine and Palm Beach.

In January 1903, *McClure's Magazine* would hit the newsstands with three powerful exposés and an editor's note that emphasized their significance. The issue contained Ida Tarbell's second installment of The History of the Standard Oil Company. Ida Tarbell, one of McClure's most influential writers, created in her series the type of influential exposé the magazine became recognized for instigating. Her investigation was grounded in a thorough history of Standard Oil. Her indictments against Rockefeller were driven by incontrovertible fact. She accused Rockefeller and his associates of systemically regulating the price of crude and refined oil. She detailed how the company controlled the refineries' output and the pricing and means of transportation for the oil. Her articles proved that Rockefeller was determined to destroy all competition and monopolize a basic commodity.

Flagler's legacy

As yesterday's tightfisted corporate villains transformed themselves into charitable philanthropists, reviled robber barons were newly christened as revered patrons. Henry Flagler reinvented himself from one of the nation's oil slicks into Florida's patron saint. With no experience as a real estate developer but with an unrivaled expertise in creating oil and railroad monopolies, Flagler converted Florida's East Coast into a packaged resort network while turning Palm Beach's jungle lakefront into an international destination.

More than a century later, although Henry Flagler's descendants remain the island's dominant historical personage from among the Standard Oil Trust of 1887's major stockholders, there were a considerable number of colleagues and their families who trailed after him.

Flagler's estranged relationship with his only son, Harry Harkness Flagler, kept them apart until Flagler's last days. He didn't visit Palm Beach for many years until his father had already lapsed into a coma. And since the Flagler railroad and hotel empire was inherited by the Kenans, Flagler's third wife's family, Harry Flagler and his wife heiress Anne Lamont Flagler spent much

---

(Left): The Bingham family scrapbook includes original images of Figulus shortly after it was built. Placed in the National Register of Historic Places in 1972, Figulus was demolished in 1974. *(Historical Society of Palm Beach County)*

of his Standard Oil stock inheritance supporting the New York Symphony, later known as the New York Philharmonic. But, it would be Harry's daughter Jean Louise Flagler who would ensure the Flagler family stamp on the island would not be forgotten.

At the age of three, after her grandfather Henry M. Flagler died in 1913, Jean Flagler inherited her first $1 million in Standard Oil stock. Thirty years later, her holdings were worth more than $9 million. By 1952, the year her father Harry Harkness Flagler died, the trust had appreciated to about $17 million. At that time, she came into another trust under his will and two other trusts from her mother, Annie Lamont Flagler. In November 1957, her $42 million trust reached its highest value, consisting of oil securities valued at $32.4 million in addition to real estate and tax-exempt municipal bonds.

In 1960, Jean Flagler Matthews led the campaign to restore Whitehall, the Palm Beach mansion built by her grandfather. She made generous charitable donations in Palm Beach, including gifts to Palm Beach Private School and The Episcopal Church of Bethesda-by-the-Sea. She died the same year that Palm Beach established its Landmark Preservation Commission, twenty years after she had taken the initiative to save one of the town's most architecturally significant buildings.

Rockefeller scions

While there were a greater number of Rockefeller descendants, none made a more lasting impact than Henry Flagler. John D. Rockefeller, Sr. preferred spending winters at the Hotel Bon Air in Augusta, Georgia. There is only one reported mention of Rockefeller ever visiting Palm Beach. According to a February 16, 1901 story in *The New York Times* headlined "New Yorkers in Florida," J. D. and William Rockefeller, accompanied by family members, arrived at the Royal Poinciana Hotel in their private rail car. Rockefeller and his entourage remained overnight in the private car before proceeding north. It does not mention if Rockefeller and Flagler, whose Whitehall mansion was well under construction at the time, met.

(Left) Top Left: Lillian Bostwick Phipps, far right, at the track. "No one loved her horses like she did," remarked one of her long-time trainers. *(Palm Beach Daily News)*

(Left) Top Right: Harry Harkness Flagler. *(Courtesy New York Philharmonic)*

(Left) Bottom: Lillian Bostwick McKim Phipps at The Society of the Four Arts in Palm Beach. *(Palm Beach Daily News)*

Although William Rockefeller was known to have spent several weeks during the 1900 season at The Royal Poinciana Hotel, he preferred the more exclusive Jekyll Island Club where he maintained a cottage, Indian Mound. William Rockefeller and Standard Oil trustee Oliver Burr Jennings were married to sisters. The Jennings family was more closely associated with the Jekyll Island Club, where Walter Jennings was president. But a descendant, Lawrence K. Jennings, lived in Palm Beach for many years.

While the Rockefeller's patriarchs may not have ever taken to Palm Beach, several family members had a notable presence. The Winston Guests hosted Winthrop Rockefeller and Bobo Sears' midnight wedding in 1948, making front page news. Though the couple separated two years later, the ceremony's peculiar circumstances kept Palm Beach in the news for longer than the duration of the marriage. Bessie Rockefeller Strong's daughter, dance patron Elizabeth Strong de Cuevas, retained several Palm Beach residences during the more than forty years she spent in Palm Beach.

In 1931, Muriel McCormick Hubbard, daughter of Edith Rockefeller McCormick, made her dramatic stage debut in the role as Mona Lisa at the Palm Beach Playhouse, where for several seasons she underwrote the theater's expenses. Muriel was in Palm Beach engaging in a highly publicized ghost marriage. In an after-dinner ceremony at Casa Alejandro on Vita Serena, she married the ghost of Chicago friend Marion McKinlock's son, who had died in World War I.

Two of Rockefeller's descendants formed their own private club. JD's grandson Spelman Prentice, whose mother Alta Rockefeller had married lawyer E. Parmalee Prentice, organized the La Coquille Club in Manalapan. A North Lake Way resident, Prentice built the oceanfront playground in 1952. Five years later, just south of La Coquille, William E. Benjamin II bought the fifty-acre estate Casa Alva from the Jacques Balsans and formed the Manalapan Club. Benjamin was the great-grandson of Standard Oil partner Henry H. Rogers.

(Left) Top Left and Right: Rockefeller family heraldry and portrait of Henry Flagler. In 1890, the Chicago Tribune wrote, "The wonder of the century is the growth of the fortunes of the Standard Oil crowd, as they are known, the Rockefellers, the Flaglers and their associates ..." *The New York Times* described Standard's elite more simply "...the most powerful, the most resourceful and the most daring combination of capitalists the country has ever known."

(Left) Bottom: Opened in 1894, Henry Flagler's Royal Poinciana Hotel made Palm Beach an international destination as well as a sheltered place for Standard Oil trustees to park their railroad cars for the winter season. The six-story Colonial-style resort attained unrivaled success, rapidly expanding into the world's largest wooden structure. With accommodations for more than 1,200 guests extending seven blocks, the resort afforded golf, tennis, canasta, yachting, and cakewalks. The hotel's lush tea garden, the Cocoanut Grove, became the island's social center offering afternoon outdoor dancing. *(Library of Congress)*

Palm Beach Standards

Without the name recognition of a Flagler or a Rockefeller, Jabez Bostwick, Standard Oil's first treasurer, made the family fortune, thus allowing his descendants to make a name for themselves. Bostwick, fashion icon Lilly Pulitzer's great-grandfather, died after he was overcome with excitement at his Mamaroneck estate following a stable fire. His neighbor, Standard Oil co-trustee, William Rockefeller, was among the first to extend condolences.

With an estimated fortune in excess of $12 million, Bostwick was an early supporter of women's rights, believing women deserved equal educational and professional opportunities. His daughter Nellie pursued dressmaking, his daughter Frances was a clinical researcher and surgeon. While his son Albert C. Bostwick was a sportsman, it was AC's descendants who achieved notable additions to several of the sporting world's halls of fame. George H. "Pete" Bostwick was a remarkable steeplechase rider before becoming a polo legend. His sister, and Lilly Pulitzer's mother, Lillian Bostwick McKim Phipps, was a prominent horse breeder and in the pantheon of croquet players.

On Cleveland's Euclid Avenue, news among other Standard Oil families must have spread quickly about Henry Flagler's acquisitions on Lake Worth and plans for Palm Beach. In 1893, the year before the Royal Poinciana Hotel opened, Mary Payne Bingham and Charles W. Bingham paid $11,000 for a one hundred sixty-acre ocean-to-lake tract in the South End. By the following fall, the *Tropical Sun* newspaper reported, "Mr. Coburn, architect for Charles Bingham arrived Monday night… he will remain several days to confer with Mr. Lainhart concerning the building of the Binghams' new residence at Figulus, which is progressing very rapidly." Forrest A. Coburn was a Cleveland architect with the Coburn & Barnum firm, associated with the design of several Euclid Avenue mansions.

At Figulus, the Bingham family pursued the carefree pleasures of sunrise swims and sunset sails. Renowned botanist Dr. David Fairchild selected and supervised the plantings, sheltered stands of towering hardwood with surrounding vegetable and ornamental gardens, fruit orchards, and wild orchids. To the east, a magnificent two thousand five hundred-foot oceanfront was buffered by a sweep of Australian pines, coconut palms and seagrapes. A stately aleé of royal palms led to a chain of mangrove islands along the lake front.

(Right): Liza Pulitzer with her mother, fashion icon Lilly McKim Pulitzer, a great-granddaughter of Jabez Bostwick and daughter of Lillian Bostwick Phipps. *(Palm Beach Daily News)*

Mrs. Bolton Betty C.W.B.
Edith Mrs. Rhodes Mr. Rhodes

In 1919, Charles W. Bingham conveyed Figulus, along with seventeen acres, to his daughter, Elizabeth Bingham Blossom. To his other daughter, Frances Bingham Bolton, he deeded the parcel to the south at 1298 South Ocean Boulevard, where Casa Apava was built. It was designed by Cleveland architect J. Abram Garfield.

The Henry Huttleston Rogers family may have been latecomers compared to the Binghams, but they were no less established in Palm Beach circles. At the time of his death Rogers left an estimated estate of more than $50 million to his four children: Henry H. Rogers Jr., and three daughters, Mrs. William E. Benjamin, Mrs. Urban Broughton and Mrs. William Coe.

But it was granddaughter Millicent Rogers who garnered the family headlines.

During the 1920s she fled from her husband in Europe to the safety of her parents' South Ocean Boulevard home. Or, so she thought. Styled then as Countess Salm van Hoogstraten, she and her sixteen-month-old son arrived accompanied by a horde of international press. The rumors and innuendoes were enough to keep Palm Beach in the national headlines for weeks. The local newspaper claimed the town's "aristocratic quietude" had been shattered.

As Count Salm checked in to the Royal Poinciana Hotel to contest the divorce, the countess claimed there had been an attempted kidnapping. Tabloid headlines barked, "Salm pa woos, Grandma cries, Pa and Cops Row." Concerned with her safety, the Countess rented La Chosa, the South End Pillsbury estate, hiring private detectives and security guards to surround her. Despite making numerous allegations against his wife, eventually Count Salm accepted a settlement from his father-in-law. He returned to Europe without his wife and son but with offers of work from the island's real estate firms who were impressed by the publicity he generated. Two marriages later, Millicent Rogers settled in New Mexico, where she became a noted style and fashion icon.

During the two decades Henry Morgan Tilford was associated with Standard Oil, he accumulated an estimated $20 million fortune. Immortalized in the film *There Will be Blood*, Tilford served as president and vice-president of various Standard Oil companies, best known for organizing

(Left) Top: The Bingham family members and their friends congregate on the porch at Figulus. The Binghams' son, Oliver Perry Bingham, whose health the family hoped would be improved by Florida's climate, died in 1900. *(Historical Society of Palm Beach County)*

(Left) Bottom: Elizabeth "Betty" Bingham, left, and her friends at Figulus, c. 1895. *(Historical Society of Palm Beach County)*

Standard Oil's west coast operation, later known as Chevron. While the Tilfords were entrenched in the social depths of Tuxedo Park, they spent several seasons at the Royal Poinciana Hotel before becoming regulars at one of The Breakers' oceanfront cottages. The Tilford daughters married within their social class — Katharine married Stanley Mortimer; Isabelle wed David Wagstaff; and Annette hitched Amory Haskell. Each of them also became part of the Standard Oil extended family that made Palm Beach their winter home.

As much as Standard Oil president and John D. Rockefeller's Tarrytown neighbor John Dustin Archbold's family made Thomasville's hunt country their preferred destination, family members also settled in Palm Beach. Archbold's $25 million estate, of which $15 million was held in Standard Oil of New Jersey stock, was equally divided between his wife and their three children, Annie, John Foster, and Mary Archbold Van Beuren. In Thomasville, John Foster Archbold built Chinquapin, a several thousand-acre hunting preserve. To the south in Lake Placid, his son, noted explorer Richard Archbold, established the Archbold Biological Station. His daughter Frances Archbold Hufty built a house on Island Road in the 1930s and remained a significant presence on Palm Beach for more than seven decades.

Among Henry Flagler's earliest boosters and partners, Pennsylvania oilman and Standard trustee William Grey Warden was among the first to follow Flagler to St. Augustine. He was a founder of the St. Augustine Improvement Association and a director of the local utility companies. In 1887, Warden built Warden's Castle, now home to the Ripley's Believe It or Not tourist attraction. Among Warden's ten children who shared his more than $10 million estate, son William G. Warden II made North Ocean Boulevard his seasonal retreat from Philadelphia winters. It was one of architect Addison Mizner's most fully-realized mansions. The Warden House, albeit now apportioned into condominiums, endures as an integral part of the island's architectural history.

But it was Warden's granddaughter, Elizabeth Donnell Kay, who perhaps made the most prolific contributions to Palm Beach. A winter resident for sixty-four years, Elizabeth and her husband Alfred Kay were among the island's most active residents, founders of St. Mary's Hospital and the Palm Beach Day School. Alfred Kay served as president of the Civic Association, The Society of the Four Arts, and the Everglades Club.

(Right): Millicent Rogers, the former Countess Salm, with her son, left, Peter Salm, and his newly-born half-brother Arturo Ramos. Following her publicized divorce, she wed Arturo Ramos in Paris. Later, she married Ronald Balcom. A style and fashion icon, she was named to the Best-Dressed list in 1940. Millicent Rogers spent her final years in Taos, New Mexico. *(Historical Society of Palm Beach County)*

For more than two decades, Elizabeth Kay was editor of the Garden Club of America's national journal. Following the well-received publication of their book, *The Plant World in Florida* in 1933, Elizabeth and Alfred Kay were the acknowledged co-writers of botanist David Fairchild's autobiography, *The World Was My Garden, Travels of a Plant Explorer*. While recognized for the artful design of their own Palm Beach houses along South Ocean Boulevard, Audita and Ananda, the couple established their own one-hundred-acre "experimental garden," which later became the Pine Jog Environmental Center. Today, Pine Jog, often supported by Elizabeth Kay's close friend and Standard Oil heir, the late Frances Archbold Hufty, is under the auspices of Florida Atlantic University. It is considered among the nation's leading environmental educational research sites.

Henry Flagler never accumulated the wealth, international standing or philanthropic magnanimity achieved by John D. Rockefeller. And yet, the history and lives of the vast web of interconnected Standard Oil families that Flagler's resort attracted were essential in developing the heart of Palm Beach.

Above: Warden House, east elevation. Designed by Addison Mizner for Standard Oil heir William Gray Warden, the landmarked Warden House at 112 Seminole Avenue was converted into condominiums.

(Left) Top: Elizabeth Donnell Kay, pictured right, was William Gray Warden's granddaughter. Her uncle, W. G. Warden Jr., built the Warden House on North Ocean Boulevard at Seminole Avenue. *(Palm Beach Daily News)*

(Left) Bottom: Elizabeth Kay made headlines when she erected a wall between her property and her neighbor, Harold S. Vanderbilt.

Mizner apprenticed and trained with California architect Willis Polk, was licensed in four states, and counted New York and Palm Beach's wealthiest people among his clients.

Envisioning Palm Beach

The Addison Mizner Collection at The Society of the Four Arts

Architect Addison Mizner's extensive library, volumes that span three centuries, and his design diaries, scrapbooks comprised of sketches, watercolors, photographs and ephemera, are noteworthy facets of the Gioconda and Joseph King Library's decorative arts collections at The Society of the Four Arts. This significant archival resource documents Mizner's influential status as a professional architect, recording a lifetime of inspiration for the houses, buildings and interiors he created, especially in New York and Palm Beach.

Because of the generosity of Amy Phipps Guest, The King Library acquired the three-hundred-volume book collection in 1940. The scrapbooks arrived nearly a decade later. When these important scholarly materials are assessed with the Historical Society of Palm Beach's collection of Mizner's architectural drawings and office records, they clearly establish him as a well-respected

---

(Left) Top: The Gilded Age grandeur of Venice's Hotel Bauer, seen in a photograph from the Addison Mizner Collection at The Society of the Four Arts in Palm Beach. Although best known for all things Spanish, Mizner frequently visited Italy, taking his first visit trip to Venice shortly after he moved to New York in 1904.

(Left) Middle Left : Addison Cairns Mizner (1872-1933).

(Left) Middle Right: First Edition Addison Mizner.

(Left) Bottom Left: Fireplace mantle sketch. Addison Mizner, architect. The Society of the Four Arts Collection.

(Left) Bottom Right: Mizner Industries lantern.

professional. He apprenticed and trained with California architect Willis Polk, was licensed in four states, and counted New York and Palm Beach's wealthiest people among his clients. Even so, Mizner's legacy was subject to disparaging assessments following his death in 1933.

Certainly, it is possible the lack of recognition for creating what became known as the Palm Beach style can be explained by Mizner's lack of formal Beaux-Arts education or his own self-effacing dinner-table wit and character, expressed in his book, *The Many Mizners*. However, without question, Alva Johnson's inane book, *The Legendary Mizners*, published in 1953 following a series of *New Yorker* magazine articles titled *The Palm Beach Architect*, did much to undermine Mizner's rank among the pantheon of American architects.

As the late architectural historian Donald Curl wrote in his authoritative book *Mizner's Florida, American Resort Architecture*, Alva Johnson's book was mistakenly classified non-fiction, as the author "retold the myths and discarded the significant architectural and cultural accomplishments." Johnson overlooked the fact that Addison Mizner was a licensed and registered architect in California, New York, Pennsylvania and Florida. Following three years of formal training with California's prominent architect Willis Polk, Mizner opened his own office in San Francisco. From 1904 until 1918, Mizner was a prominent New York architect and interior designer before moving to Palm Beach.

The social climb

Johnson's influential unexacting anecdotes became the dubious standard for appraising Mizner's talents, including the unshakable myths about the architect's ability to design staircases.

Despite the aesthetic and structural harmony of Mizner's varied stairways, for the past seventy years critics and colleagues continue to mock the architect's designs as "staircases to nowhere" and "forgotten staircases." Perhaps taking its cue from Johnson's book, a 1969 *Palm Beach Post* article stumbled when it said Mizner's design for Casa Nana "neglected to put in a staircase between the first and second floor. Not wanting to impair the aesthetic value, Mizner installed a staircase on the outside of the house."

(Right): At Louwana, the Mizner-designed Venetian-inspired open staircase is the focal point of the courtyard.

In fact, Mizner included exterior open European-styled staircases in several of his Palm Beach houses, including Casa Bendita, Louwana and La Fontana, built when air-conditioning consisted of a sea breeze. Designed in 1926 for George Rasmussen, Casa Nana was among Mizner's last great Palm Beach mansions, making the staircase slip-up stories even more dubious. However, it remains the legend most often believed in today's world of central air-conditioned entrance halls.

"At Casa Nana, Addison Mizner began with the open tower and designed the house around it," said Curl, who interviewed Lester Geisler, Mizner's draftsman who completed the working drawings for the house.

As Curl pointed out, "The tower shelters the entrance," making preposterous the repeated fiction that Mizner completely forgot staircases.

Mizner experts still have difficulty detecting authentic 16th-century Renaissance antiquities from the reproductions and facsimiles manufactured at Mizner Industry's factory in West Palm Beach. "Mizner's staircases remain convincing expressions of the architect's enduring unmistakable brilliance," Curl said.

The enormous scope and extent of the Mizner library and scrapbooks make evident the work of an articulate seasoned architect versed on a wide spectrum of subjects, international in reach. The collection includes the two-volume set of Andrae Putei's *Perspectiva pictorum et architectuorum*, published in 1723. It also includes Spanish and Italian publications used by Mizner Industries to manufacture historically accurate furnishings and fixtures in the 1920s.

In addition to architectural theory, practice and history, there are detailed reference volumes on building construction, civil engineering, structural engineering, landscape architecture, interior design and decoration, the decorative arts and town planning. Plus, the collection affords rare glimpses of Europe's glorious architectural wonders before they were destroyed by World War I. A scenic picturesque culture devised by classically-schooled ateliers more accustomed to pencil-and-ink sketches than photography. Mizner amassed an impressive array of images — turn-of-the-century Venetian watercolors, Baroque altarpieces, Venetian chimneys, Castilian convents, and Byzantine ceilings.

(Left): At Casa Nana, Addison Mizner designed the open staircase as the focal point. *(Historical Society of Palm Beach County)*

The scrapbooks are catalogued according to geography, historical period and by subject matter. Each volume is more than one hundred pages, composed of sketches, small-format personal travel photographs and large-format professional photographs, postcards, tear sheets and booklets, making for as many as thirty thousand images. *Spain and the Colonies* is a three-volume set featuring what may be every plaza, calle, avenida and iglesia in Spain, Mexico, Cuba and Guatemala. Rome and Venice are combined into one volume. Historical period categories include Aztec and Primitive, Byzantine, Moorish and Near East, Gothic and Romanesque.

In referencing the assembly-line of furnishings and accessories manufactured by his Mizner Industries factory, descriptive subject headings provide the historic models and production guidelines. These include: Ironwork and Fixtures, Woodwork and Furniture, Fireplaces, Chimneys, and Ceilings, Murals, Panels and Doors, and especially artful, a heading titled Costumes and Portraits. A nine-volume set of *Arte y Decoracion en Espana, 1917-1926*, includes images of the authentic period artifacts and furniture manufactured by Mizner Industries.

In today's Palm Beach, there are only about forty of Addison Mizner's houses and buildings remaining in various forms. Some of Mizner's most significant works, including Playa Riente, La Florencia, and Casa Bendita, were demolished during the late 1950s and 1970s when Palm Beach could not resist the sophistication of subdivisions and condominiums.

The Addison Mizner Collection at The Society of the Four Arts is one of Palm Beach's key resources in appreciating how Palm Beach was envisioned nearly a century ago.

(Left): A Mizner-designed staircase at Casa Florencia for the Preston Satterwhites. *(Historical Society of Palm Beach County)*

Palm Beach Life, magazine cover.

Preserving the Status Quo – 1930s Palm Beach

In January 1931, Mrs. Charles Hall entertained guests with what was then described as a "novel amusement." Guests dressed in their finest pajamas and sipped champagne as they moved around the backyard of her El Bravo Way villa, their movements based on a throw of dice on a fifty-foot canvas painted to resemble a backgammon board.

Despite the rest of the nation's despair and pessimism brought on by the onset of the Great Depression, for some Palm Beachers, as immune from the economic setbacks as the Halls, life was still more about finger bowls than the Dust Bowl. During the previous decade, Palm Beach's social profile had escalated from the Flagler-era's established programed resort life to a more permissive and private dusk-til-dawn laissez-faire extravagance. The emergence of the Cottage Colony and private clubs had shifted the town's social axis away from commonplace hotel rotundas and just another night at Bradley's gambling tables.

"There has been a crash and a big one. But we're still carrying on, if Palm Beach may be used as a criterion," said E.W. Kamelbert, a Wall Street expert and guest at the Royal Poinciana Hotel during the 1930 season. Kamelbert added that he saw America getting "bigger and better, as evidenced in this resort."

However much the winter colony acted at ease, unruffled by a stock market crash and real-estate bust, it could not escape fallout from the devastating Hurricane of 1928. The usually composed resort landscape was touched with more than scattered coconuts and cracked sea walls. Palm Beach's inclination toward excess was tempered and recast during the 1930s without losing its proclivity for paradox.

Nonetheless, as streamlined Pullman sleeping cars arrived with visitors ready for Palm Beach soirees where black-tie and white dinner-jackets became the required formalwear, Dust Bowl denizens and freight-train hobos became the nation's recurring image. The Chamber of Commerce reported that "Palm Beach was enjoying one of its largest seasons." National unemployment reached twenty-five percent and as many as five thousand banks had failed. On South County Road, the First National Bank recorded assets of $4.5 million and offered savings accounts at four percent interest, welcoming new accounts with as little as a dollar.

In January 1930, the town's councilmen deliberated over a projected annual budget of $210,000. Between matters of lot clearing and sea wall repairs, as well as concerns over a shortfall caused by homeowners' delinquent payment of taxes, town leaders budgeted $4,000 for administrative work, $6,100 for the police department and $7,200 for the fire department. The same month, the town established a seven-member planning commission, as recommended by the Garden Club of Palm Beach's plan.

Both the FEC and Seaboard Air Line railroads reported increased bookings. Real estate brokers said there was "unusual demand for small apartments." Included among the more than $3 million in building permits issued in 1930, sportsman Joseph Widener moved forward on the construction of Il Palmetto, described as Palm Beach's "largest and most elaborate in years." Additionally, with passage of Florida's pari-mutuel bill in 1931, Widener and his Palm Beach partners reopened Hialeah Park as one of the nation's racing showplaces.

The Breakers beauty salon advertised a fashionable "Croquignole Wave." As Howard Lanin's orchestra played nightly for the hotel's guests, much of cafe society preferred the resort's more intimate European-styled nightclubs. The Patio's starlit dance floor and The Colony Club's gardens attracted large throngs. The Embassy Club on Royal Palm Way was filled to overflowing.

The Palm Beach Country Club continued to host local and state golf tournaments. Tennis round robins and deep-sea fishing pursuits still made front-page news. The Oasis Club's weekly "boxing teas" attracted as many as five hundred social heavyweights. The island's colorful Romany Chorus added comedy skits to its previously staid costumed productions. At the Jardin Bijou on Worth

(Left): On Prize Night, The Patio nightclub on North County Road was one of Palm Beach's most popular nightclubs during the 1930s. Above, Isabel Dodge Sloane, Peggy Seyburn, and Ellen Glendinning Frazer arrive for an evening of uninhibited fun. *(Lucius Ordway Frazer Collection)*

Avenue, Pooshie-Pooshie entertained after the nightly balloon dance. The Berlin-Griff package store offered twenty-four-hour delivery.

Along the Midtown municipal beach, the scene was described as "a mass of color and activity where visitors enjoyed sun tanning." The Chamber of Commerce declared that "not a single link in the chain of information indicates Palm Beach is experiencing anything other than one of its largest seasons ever."

Club matters

And yet, over at the Everglades Club its three hundred members were proceeding cautiously. The once exclusive private club was in receivership. Foreclosure proceedings were threatened. The club's bon vivant owner, Paris Singer, had mortgaged the club property to fuel his speculative real estate ventures that were in various stages of legal ambiguity. Singer fled the country as one of his sons took over the presidency.

According to a club history written by Austin B. Rittenour and published during the 1970s, Everglades Club dues for couples were lowered from $200 to $150. Ned Stotesbury suggested not holding the annual ball because publicity would make it appear they were "spending money foolishly." Dinner prices were set at $4; for gala nights, the dinner tab was raised to $5. When the charge was later raised to $6, members complained; the management relented and rescinded the raise when they saved a dollar by excluding the cost of one entree option from the menu.

At one point, the Everglades Club considered opening the Orange Gardens to the public between 10 p.m. and 2 a.m. According to Rittenour's "official history," the concept was quashed by the bankruptcy judge who feared it would detract from the club's ultimate value. Instead, members were issued invitation cards allowing their guests to use the club facilities between 10 p.m. and 2 a.m., except Thursdays and Sundays.

(Right) Top: Worth Avenue, c. 1935. The Cartier shop on the corner of Worth Avenue and Hibiscus Avenue. *(Library of Congress)*

(Right) Bottom: Worth Avenue, c. 1935. *(Library of Congress)*

During the mid-1930s, the club emerged from its tenuous financial predicament when a group of members purchased the facilities, organized as the Everglades Protective Syndicate. A decade later, the Everglades Club became a totally member-owned club.

Restraint to recovery

During the spring of 1933, a national economic recovery was widely reported. By December, Palm Beach hotels were eighty percent booked and more than two hundred thirty shops and businesses awaited the forthcoming winter season, touting soufflés and sodas, diamonds and dial phones, and cottages and castles.

Specialty grocers such as J.H. Butterfield Co. of Bar Harbor, Southampton Market, Irving Company, Aiello's Market and Bustani's advertised "fresh caviar daily" and delicacies from Europe and Asia. On Peruvian Avenue and County Road, the Cadillac showroom displayed the latest V-16 model. The Chocolate Soda Bar's counter stools were filled. Bakeries and specialty shops flourished, including a nut shop. While the windows at the Beaux Arts chic shops resembled many at Rockefeller Plaza, only steps away on Main Street, Wo-Kee's Chinese restaurant was serving plates of chop suey.

In the September 1934 issue of *House Beautiful* magazine, local historian Louis Capron wrote an article titled "Revolt in Palm Beach." Capron described how Palm Beach had abandoned Spanish and Italian motifs, extolling the virtues of the reserved functional Tropical Colonial architectural style. At the same time, Jacques Balsan and his wife, the former Consuelo Vanderbilt and the one-time Duchess of Marlborough, announced plans to build a "palatial residence" on Hypoluxo Island.

But, as much as Capron praised Howard Major and Marion Wyeth's designs as "houses to be lived in rather than for their theatrical qualities," Palm Beach could still not resist being a stage

(Right) Top Left: Palm Beach *Social Register*, 1933. *(Palm Beach Daily News)*

(Right) Top Right: Robert Glendinning, a Philadelphia financier, was one of the Everglades Club board members who during the 1930s formed a syndicate that bought the club and its property holdings from a bankruptcy court. *(Lucius Ordway Frazer Collection)*

(Right) Bottom: In 1931, wheelchairs were still a popular mode of transport on Palm Beach. The Glendinning children head over to El Mirasol where Eva Stotesbury has invited the children to visit their private zoo. *(Lucius Ordway Frazer Collection)*

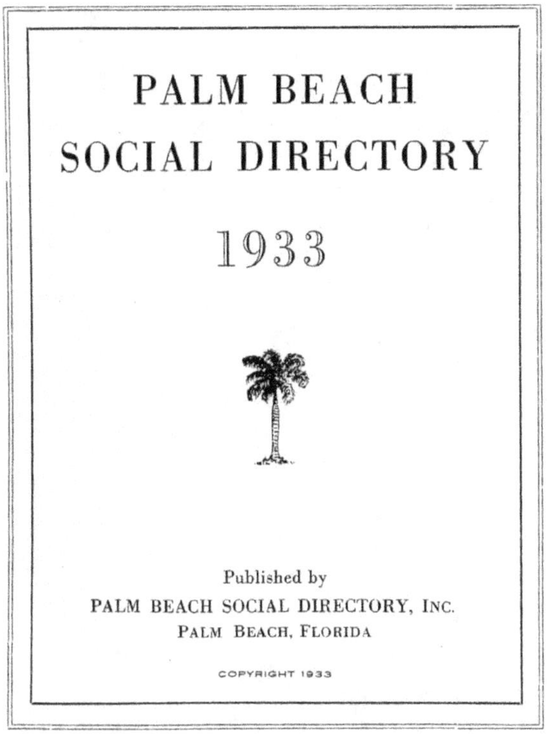

PALM BEACH
SOCIAL DIRECTORY
1933

Published by
PALM BEACH SOCIAL DIRECTORY, INC.
PALM BEACH, FLORIDA

COPYRIGHT 1933

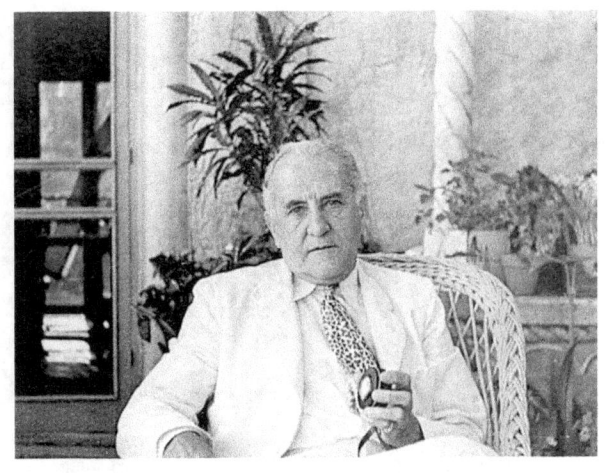

During the spring of 1933,
a national economic recovery
was widely reported.

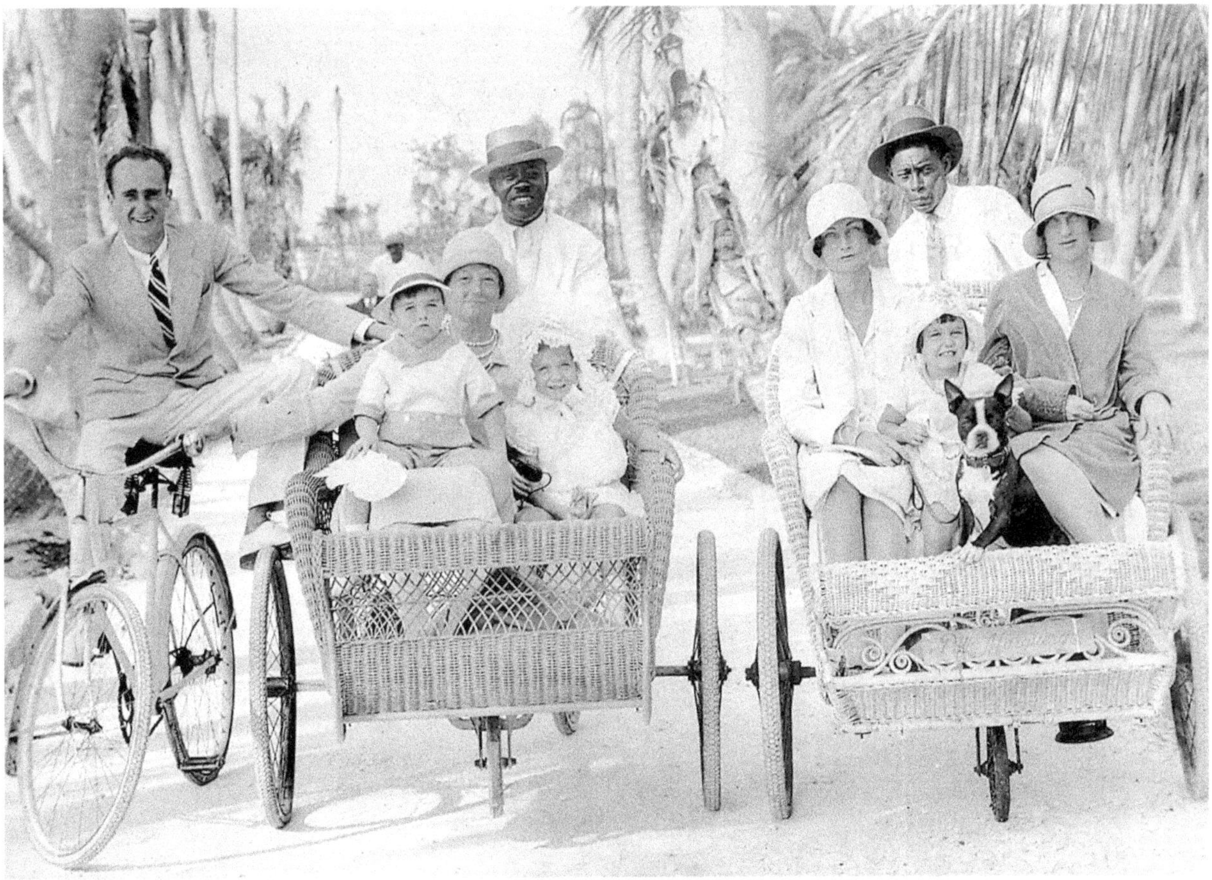

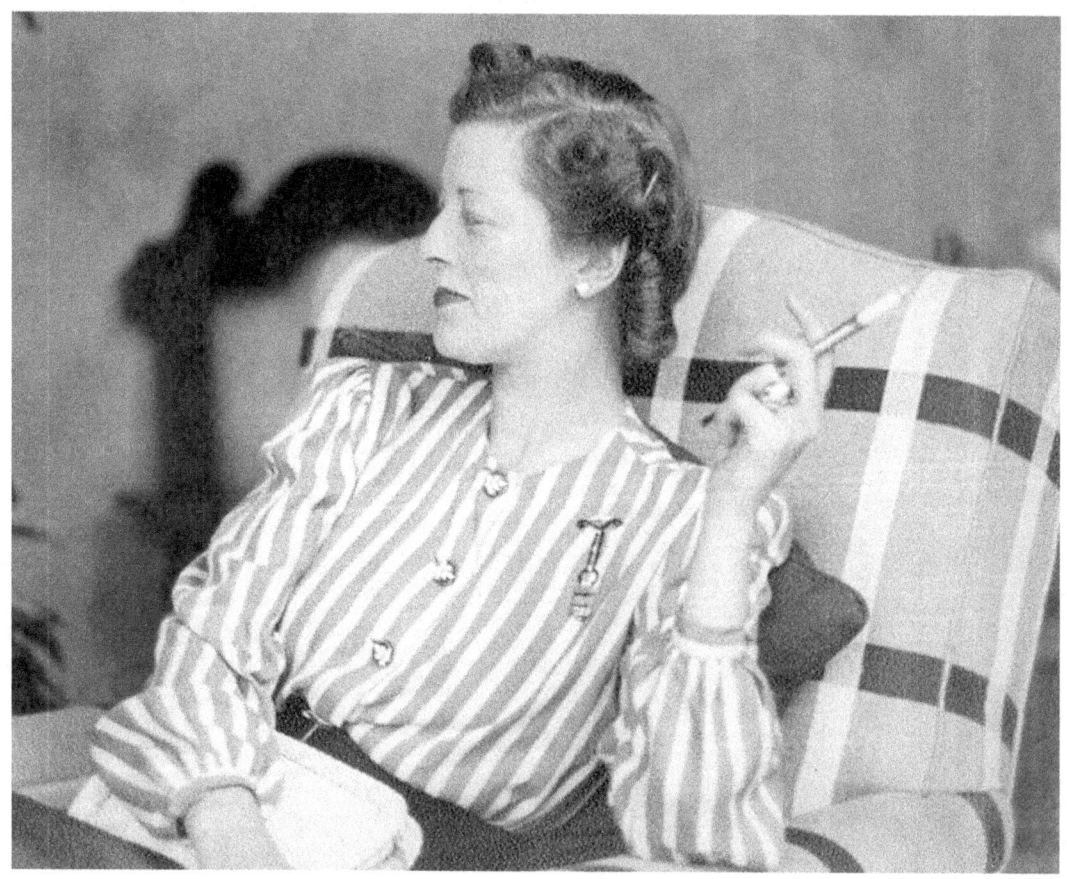

for the incomparable. The Garden Club's 1934 three-day show at the Royal Poinciana Hotel's Slat House featured a re-creation of Rome's Piazza di Spagna, the largest display ever produced.

The following year, the Everglades Club staged a Bal de Tête fundraiser for Good Samaritan Hospital where four hundred guests arrived in their Hispano-Suiza Cabriolets and Packard Phaetons with elaborate headdresses. Showman and Palm Beach resident George Jessel was emcee for the "unusually striking" event; Mrs. Jessel, better known as Norma Talmadge, starred in the benefit's pageant *The Pirate Returns*. Following a Parade de Tête at 11 p.m., where judges awarded prizes to the most original coiffures, orchestras and musicians from Palm Beach clubs and hotels performed during what was called "Palm Beach passes through the Everglades Club."

This "far-into-the-night" affair set a new standard for benefits, marking Palm Beachers' spirited robust character and making for one of Palm Beach's most unforgettable moments.

(Left) Top: Perkie Frazer greets his family riding in their Palm Beach wheelchair. Pictured are his grandmother Elizabeth Glendinning (seated right), her daughter-in-law Kitty Glendinning, and at the wheel, Robert Glendinning Jr. *(Lucius Ordway Frazer Collection)*

(Left) Bottom: The 1930s-era style is modeled by Mary Spain Floyd-Jones Weston, New York, Southampton and Palm Beach, at a dinner given by Stephen and Mary Sanford at the Sanford family's Villa Marina. The former Mrs. Roy Floyd-Jones, Mary Spain married Herb Weston in 1927. *(Lucius Ordway Frazer Collection)*

Royal Palm Beach

Palm Beach's eclectic social aristocracy has always welcomed a visiting tiara and crowned head, regaled by their titled provenance whether to the manor born, bought, married, or forged, styled as peers, demi-royals, semi-royals, or no-account counts.

The tropical beachhead is a coveted destination on the treasure map of gilded watering holes for all manner of lords and ladies. Palm Beach has never attracted the number of Sirs and Ladies found along the English and French Riviera, places the far-flung coconut-palmed island once emulated. The platinum sandbar remains a part of the Southern Colonies, however much some still consider it a self-governing duchy, city-state or offshore kingdom once ruled by a solitary social queen.

Unlike its European counterparts where every other table might claim some allusion to royaldom, Palm Beach hosts leaped at the prospect of having a suave baron grace their receiving lines, no matter the cobwebs that might be holding together the family castle. The touch of class afforded by visiting titles assured a sense of incomparable exclusiveness to the most mundane charity ball.

At Whitehall, the Henry Flaglers' southern-styled Beaux Arts mansion, the guest list included Count and Countess Szechneyi as well as the visiting Duke of Abruzzi. With its Parisian chef and Monte Carlo-style roulette wheel, Col. Bradley's Beach Club fabricated continental ambience on the North Lake Trail only added to the fantasy of the Duke and Duchess of Sutherland's visit to Palm Beach. In more recent history, with many historically feudal titles becoming available

(Left): The Duke and Duchess of Windsor's annual Palm Beach visits created such a social whirl it was called its own "Mini Season". *(Palm Beach Daily News)*

because of a land transfer, more authentic stately royals such as King Hussein, Maharani of Baroda and King Saud have enhanced the resort's stately prominence.

Along with these imported grandees, some of Palm Beach's best-known debutantes and hostesses of a certain era could not resist the allure of enhancing their fortunes with titles. Barbara Hutton became a serial royalist — a countess, a baroness and a double princess. Standard Oil heiress Millicent Rogers was titled Countess von Salm-Hoogstraten. Cincinnati socialite Audrey Emery was transformed into a Russian princess. But rather than ascending the Russian throne, her son Paul Ilyinsky became one of Palm Beach's most popular mayors. Newport and Palm Beach descendant Consuelo Vanderbilt was the unhappy Duchess of Marlborough before later marrying Jacques Balsan and settling for a more demure introduction as a Madame.

Of course, Palm Beach's most celebrated royal visitors were the Duke and Duchess of Windsor, who for years were the spotlight of their own "mini-season," as their several weeks whirlwind visits were called. At the same time that King Edward VII's abdication and subsequent marriage to Bessie Wallis Warfield Spencer Simpson, a Baltimore-born twice-divorced American commoner, relegated the newly-dubbed Duke and Duchess of Windsor to the status of personae non gratae within Great Britain, the "most romantic couple in the world" reigned as social luminaries among the international Café Society set. And where better than Palm Beach to be the center of attraction?

Palm Beach embraced the chic castaways, making the sovereigns-without-a-kingdom the island's most-wanted guests. The mild-mannered man who sacrificed his crown and throne but would still be addressed as "Your Royal Highness," and his wife, who could never become queen and would never be known as "Your Highness" but always "Your Grace," were considered Palm Beach's iconic royal standard.

As early as 1937, a local headline proclaimed, "Palm Beach is considered as Windsor Home." But yet, the couple did not make their first visit until four years later, after the duke was appointed governor and commander-in-chief of the Bahamas. In Nassau, they were ensconced at Government House. The Bahamas' new First Lady began a major renovation supervised by Lady Mendl. From their official island outpost, the ducal duo traveled within the Cartier-Perrier Triangle of New York penthouses, South of France villas, and Palm Beach mansions.

Although deprived of regal trappings, they succeeded in becoming their era's "style leaders." After two decades on the best dressed list, the duchess' chic outfits were accessorized with Queen Mary's pearls and Cartier jaguars. Soon, the duchess was enshrined in the fashion world's International Hall of Fame. Even the duke's necktie knot, dubbed the Windsor knot, assured him immortality in fashion's pantheon.

For their initial plunge in April 1941 into the island's social swim, they encamped at the Everglades Club for a three-day weekend. In subsequent visits during the next thirty years, they would lodge with the island's A-list. Herbert Pulitzer, Robert and Anita Young, Christopher Dunphy, Albert Worswick, Arthur and Suzanne Gardner, and Winston and CZ Guest were among those who made sure the couple's Porthault sheets were pressed and their tea was properly steeped.

Although the Everglades Club had already closed for the season when the Duke and Duchess arrived, the club spruced up an apartment for the visiting demi-royals. A British Empire flag flew alongside the Stars and Stripes. Upon arrival, the duke held a press conference at the club. Outside, onlookers remained stationed, greeting their every egress and ingress with polite applause. Their daytime schedule would be much the same as it would be for every Palm Beach visit. The duke played golf; the duchess shopped on Worth Avenue.

((Left) Top Left: King Saud bin Abdul-Aziz, King of Saudia Arabia, welcomes President John F. Kennedy. In January 1962, King Saud rented Vita Serena, Jean Flagler Mathews' house on Clarendon Avenue. *(John F. Kennedy Presidential Library)*

(Left) Top Right: Paul Ilyinsky. Grandson of Tsar Alexander II and son of Grand Duke Dmitri Pavlovich, he became a popular mayor of Palm Beach. *(Lucius Ordway Frazer Collection)*

"I've only brought along a few refugee rags from France," she told the press during their inaugural visit, who were probably not aware the couple had checked-in with twenty pieces of luggage.

Their first stay was a whirlwind. Jessie Woolworth Donahue hosted a lunch at Cielito Lindo. Wolcott and Ellen Blair held a cocktail party. Then it was on to dinner at Casa Giraventa where Winifred Dodge Seyburn entertained them. As the couple boarded Harold Vanderbilt's seaplane for the return to Nassau, their Palm Beach outing was described by newspapers as "an epochal event." Their successive ten-day late March visits became known as Palm Beach's "little season."

"She was always upfront," recalled Brownie McLean. "I believe she made all the decisions on whether to accept or decline invitations."

Because the duchess was reluctant to fly, they usually arrived aboard the Florida Special from New York at the West Palm Beach train station, always accompanied by their French pugs. During the 1940s and 1950s, they were Robert and Anita Young's guests at their North County Road oceanfront estate, The Towers. Both couples maintained apartments at the Waldorf Towers in New York and the Windsors were also guests at Fairholme, the Youngs' estate on Newport's Cliff Walk.

If not there, they could be found at the Albert Worswicks' or the Arthur Gardners' house on South Ocean Boulevard, or at Villa Artemis as guests of the Winston Guests. Barton and Walter Gubelmann held a Hawiian luau for them.

In between servings of lemon sole and baked Alaska and cocktails at the Celebrity Room or the Club Moulin Rouge, the twosome supported their friends' charity events. During one hectic "little season," they were waltzing at the La Coquille Club's Polo Ball one night. The next night,

(Right) Top: Mary Sanford, the "Queen of Palm Beach," Stephen Sanford, and the Duke and Duchess of Windsor keep warm during a polo match. *(Palm Beach Daily News)*

(Right) Bottom Left: Dame Celia Farris and Baron Arndt Krupp von Bohlen und Halbach, the last heir to the Krupp fortune. *(Palm Beach Daily News)*

(Right) Bottom Right: Douglas Fairbanks Jr. was among Hollywood's royalty who made Palm Beach their home. *(Palm Beach Daily News)*

65

they made an appearance at a Boca Raton Club fundraiser. The following morning, the duke would tee off at a golf tournament in West Palm Beach named in his honor benefiting the Damon Runyan Cancer Fund.

During their 1954 holiday, the duke caused a stir as he entered the Palm Beach County Courthouse to renew his driver's license. When asked for his occupation, the reserved former King of England wrote, "peer of the realm."

When they returned two years later to stay on Jungle Road with Chris Dunphy, the duchess was busily writing her autobiography, *The Heart Hath its Reasons*. Although she claimed there had been no ghost writer, the previous year, social historian Cleveland Amory announced he had resigned as the duchess' paid writer because he could not turn her into "Rebecca of Sunnybrook Farm.

"She always walked in front of him rather than the other way around," recalled Jim Ponce, who was a manager at The Colony Hotel when the royal couple checked into the hotel's penthouse in the early 1960s.

In 1968, Marjorie Post, Palm Beach's own "American Empress," hosted a benefit at Mar-a-Lago with a showing of *A King's Story*, the film based on the Duke of Windsor's memoirs published in 1951.

The final wave

"We are here to visit friends not to attend balls," said the duchess when they arrived in 1970 for what would be their final Palm Beach visit.

The 1971 headline "The Duke and Duchess won't be in Palm Beach" after they had been expected, proved "... nearly enough to cause a nervous breakdown," claimed Suzy, the society chronicler. A Winthrop House apartment had been redone for them. A series of charitable events were scheduled promising their presence. But, at the last minute, they sent regrets due to ill health.

(Right): In March 1934, Nancy Yuille and Viscount Adare were married at Louwana, which her sister Ellen Blair and her husband Wolcott Blair had rented for the season while their new Treanor and Fatio-designed oceanfront house was being built on South Ocean Boulevard. Charles Munn was Lord Adare's best man. *(Lucius Ordway Frazer Collection)*

Dinner in honor of
Their Royal Highnesses
The Duke of Windsor
and The Duchess of Windsor

* * *

Consommé Royal
* *
Truite froide
* *
Pigeon au riz sauvage
Coeurs d'artichauts   Champignons
* *
Salade Printannière
* *
Fromages assortis
* *
Fraises Romanoff

April 4, 1966

In May of the following year, the duke died, ten days after being visited by Queen Elizabeth, Prince Phillip and Prince Charles. The duchess spent the next fourteen years in various stages of seclusion until her death in 1986, veritably unseen during the last six years of her life. Their titles, though buried with them, remain the touchstones for one of the world's extraordinary love stories.

The world's fascination with hereditary ruling dynasties may have long since faded, but Palm Beach has always reveled in the archaic indulgences and illusions that come with a title and a tiara's aura and ambience. The Duke and Duchess' life of exile can best be remembered by the duchess's words. Late in life, she remarked to a friend as she saw the duke walking toward her, "Here comes my romance."

(Left) Top Left: A dinner menu fit for a duke. Estée Lauder's dinner menu for the Duke and Duchess of Windsor during the 1966 season. *(Lucius Ordway Frazer Collection)*

(Left) Top Right: Barbara Hutton, Countess Haugwitz-Reventlow, photographed by Ellen Glendinning Frazer at an Everglades Club golf tournament. *(Lucius Ordway Frazer Collection)*

(Left) Bottom: 319 El Vedado was the former Palm Beach home of Mme. Consuelo Balsan, once the Duchess of Marlborough, was designed by Clarence Mack with a Tropical Empire façade.

Mr. Palm Beach – Charles Munn & Claude D. Reese

However improbable, considering Palm Beach's small town charm, two of the town's larger-than-life personalities were conferred with the same eminent title of Mr. Palm Beach. But when individuals garner as much social regard and civic respect as luminary Charles Munn and political patriarch Claude Dimick Reese, you can understand how the island honored both men with the coveted designation. And yet, however much their names might have been identical, their lives were incredibly dissimilar.

Charles Munn and his family were among the earliest families arriving by private rail car at Flagler's resorts; Claude Reese's pioneer Dimick family roots pre-dated Flagler, his family having trekked by steamship and sailboat to Lake Worth. And yet, however divergent their style, both men achieved a unique level of recognition. Munn was described as a "20th century Magnum," by Lorelle Hearst. "Elegantissimo grand seigneur," decreed Suzy, the international set's social arbiter. The Dimicks' house Orangerie was the setting for church picnics. As Palm Beach's first innkeepers at their Cocoanut Grove Hotel, Dimick-Reese family members welcomed hunters, fishermen and shell collectors.

Charles Munn's parents lived the life of top hats, walking sticks and fur coats. His father had gone to Chicago to plot the expansion of Munn, Orr & Company wholesale provisional business into the Midwest market. Instead, Charles Alexander Munn married Carrie Louise Gurnee Armour, the widow of Joseph Armour, president of Armour & Co. Attended by footmen and maids, the

(Left): Charles Munn and his daughter Frances Munn Baker. *(Lucius Ordway Frazer Collection)*

Munns left Chicago for the more cosmopolitan life found in a Washington, D.C. brick mansion at 14th Street and Massachusetts Avenue, where their neighbors were Alexander Graham Bell and Postmaster General John Wanamaker.

As they packed and unpacked steamer trunks for ocean crossings and Grand Tours, the Munns became part of Newport's social vortex. In their search of a healthy clime during the winter months, the Munns traveled to St. Augustine, the Newport of the South. They stayed at Hotel Ponce de Leon. Later, the Munns were among the first arrivals at The Royal Poinciana Hotel and The Breakers, Henry Flagler's tropical aristocratic refuge. An orchestra and mule-driven trolley car greeted guests as they arrived in private railroad cars.

During his last year at Harvard, Charles Munn II married Mary Astor Paul, named for her late aunt Mary Paul Astor, the wife of William Waldorf Astor. The new Mrs. Munn's was blue chip Philadelphia; her mother Frances Drexel was the daughter of financier Anthony J. Drexel, known as "the man who made Wall Street." In Palm Beach, Charles and Mary Paul Munn built Amado on a three-acre oceanfront parcel purchased from John S. Phipps, whose family estate, Casa Bendita, adjoined the property to the south. The Munn guest register at Amado recorded the names of some of the 20th century's most distinguished international diplomats, aristocrats and socialites.

Following his divorce in the 1930s, Charles Munn spent the next two decades dining and dancing among the black-tie international social circuit. In 1953, he exchanged vows with Dorothy Spreckels, the San Francisco sugar heiress, with whom he had enjoyed an extended companionship.

A founder of the Everglades Club, Seminole and Gulf Stream Golf Club, Charles Munn was a social lion for more than six decades, a member of *le beau monde*, Café Society, and the Jet Set. Considered "The Last Gentleman," Munn was a perennial nominee to the International Best Dressed list, credited with popularizing the blue blazer, ascot and flannel trousers as the resort's official uniform.

Munn's brother and business partner was Gurnee Munn. Louwana, the Munn-Wanamaker Palm Beach home, became an epicenter for the international set during the 1920s and 1930s. Gurnee held various positions in the family firm, American Totalisator (AmTote).

Charles and his brother Gurnee, who had married department store heiress Marie-Louise Wanamaker, the daughter of their former neighbor in Washington, were partners in various enterprises. In 1926, they went to England where they organized the Greyhound Racing Association. Within a year, there were forty greyhound racetracks that utilized the Munns' patented ubiquitous mechanical rabbit.

From there, the Munn brothers and their partners developed the automatic betting board for racetracks. Charles and Gurnee Munn formed the American Totalisator Company (AmTote). Their company introduced an electronic wagering board at Pimlico in 1930; at Hialeah Park in 1931. AmTote's automation revolutionized the racing world. During the 1940s, they also took over and ran Tropical Race Track in Miami.

With a plethora of descendants still living in Palm Beach, Charles Munn's ever stylish legacy remains a presence. Conversely, being the last direct descendant of one of Palm Beach's first families still residing on the barrier island may sound like a burdensome legacy. However, North End resident David Reese manages to elude his family's historical spotlight while still appreciating the same attractions that more than one hundred and thirty years ago brought his forbearers to the east shore of Lake Worth.

(Left) Bottom: Amado was built in Palm Beach by Charles and Mary Paul Munn. *(Collection of Anthony Baker)*

With the death in 2008 of his brother, C. Dimick Reese Jr., and his daughters opting to live elsewhere, David Reese has become the last of the Dimick-Reese family's lineage rooted on Palm Beach. The Dimick-Reese family has been at the heart of Palm Beach's history since 1876, when Reese's great-grandfather's family, the Elisha Newton "Cap" Dimicks, settled their homestead Orangerie between where The Society of the Four Arts and Whitehall are today. It was described then as "a Garden of Eden with blue skies, clear water, sweet flowers and singing birds."

"Cap" Dimick, the town's first mayor, organized the first bank, started the first drug store, opened the first hotel, The Cocoanut Grove House, and was the first president of the Lake Worth Pioneers' Association, organized in 1893. As president and co-owner of the Palm Beach Improvement Co. and as part of his Royal Park development, he built the Royal Park Bridge, the island's first public toll bridge. As a Palm Beach resident, Dimick was elected to the Florida House of Representatives and Florida Senate.

After Dimick died in 1919, his wife, Ella carried on as president of the Pioneers' Association. Ella Dimick's legacy was also recognized. In 1938, she was honored by one of the town's rare scrolled-parchment resolutions, designed no less than the architectural firm, Treanor & Fatio, in recognition of "a pioneer who aided in carving an empire out of a jungle."

"My great-grandfather made friends with the Seminoles. When they came to the island to hunt for turtle eggs, he allowed them to sleep on the front porch. You better believe, my great-grandmother Ella was frightened to death and slept with one eye open," laughed David Reese.

Reese's grandfather, Thomas Tipton "Tip" Reese, who had married Cap Dimick's daughter, Belle, managed Col. E.R. Bradley's family's extensive properties before becoming the town's second mayor, a bank president and the first treasurer of the Everglades Club. "Paris Singer gave him a membership if he would become the club's first treasurer," Reese recalled.

While these accomplishments would assure the family a prominent spot in Palm Beach's historical annals, Reese's father, Claude Dimick Reese Sr., added further to the family legacy.

(Right) Top Left: Mayor Claude Reese and his wife Jean Reese. *(Palm Beach Daily News)*

(Right) Top Right: Mayor Claude Reese advertisement as "Mr. Palm Beach." *(Palm Beach Daily News)*

(Right) Bottom: Fourth-generation Palm Beacher David Reese photographed at his home on the island's North End oceanfront.

"MR. PALM BEACH"
That's what Palm Beachers call Mayor Claude Reese

...and for very good reason!

- Mayor of Palm Beach for 17 consecutive years
- Former member of Town Council for 25 years

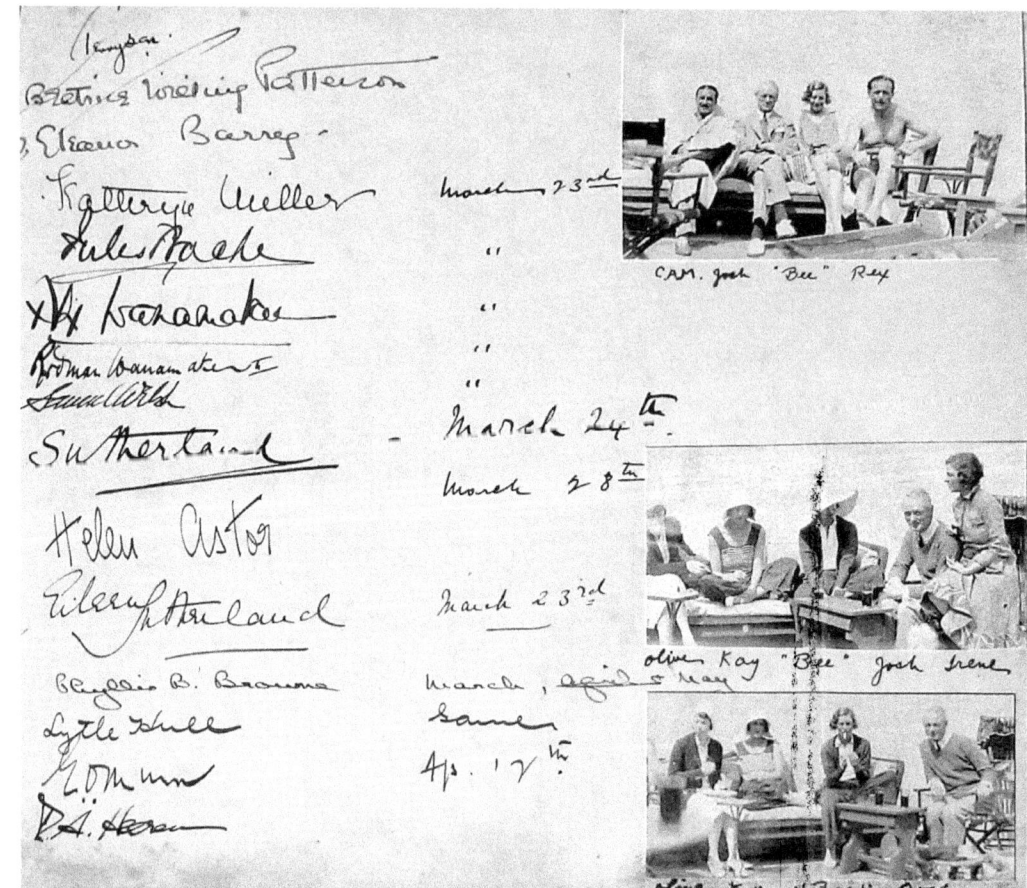

Serving more than forty years in town government, Claude Reese was mayor from 1953-70, having previously served as a town councilman from 1922-27 and council president from 1933-52.

Nonetheless, David Reese has also carried on the family tradition — but not at Town Hall.

"My father is in the East Coast Surfing Hall of Fame," said Courtenay D. Reese, about her famous surfer father, who was among the first inducted into the organization's pantheon in 1996. Being in the Surfing Hall of Fame may not be regarded as having the same stature as being a member of a mayoral dynasty, but like his pioneer predecessors, Reese played a leading role in Palm Beach's and Florida's surfing history.

As much as his family's name will always be a part of local history and he'll be known for making waves in the surfing world, Reese seems to like talking most about the island's changing nature.

"North of Tangier Avenue, the higher bluffs along the ocean were leveled, the ground pushed in to fill in the interior marshes, ponds and lagoons that once made up most of the island's North End," recalled David Reese.

"You had to cross a bridge to visit anybody who lived on the lake side. We had to cross a skinny creaky bridge across alligator-filled marsh to visit Jim Owens' house, somewhere around the end of Via Linda where the huge banyan tree was, I think."

But rather than dwell solely on long-ago Palm Beach, Reese keeps both feet planted in the present, heading a real-estate agency established in 1929 by his father. With the sale of the family's insurance business, now Celedinas-Reese Insurance, Reese and his daughter, Courtenay, are full-time real estate brokers at the Claude Reese Real Estate office, believed to be the island's oldest, now located on the ocean block of Royal Palm Way, a block east of where the agency was located for many years.

However divergent their lives, the Munn and Dimick-Reese families serve as a reminder of the vision and values that made Palm Beach a much sought-after destination.

(Left) Top: Charles Munn and his second wife Dorothy Spreckels Munn. Palm Beach, 1965. *(Lucius Ordway Frazer Collection)*

(Left) Bottom: Amado, guest book. Charles Munn's guest book registers many of the 20th century's most prominent social figures.

Playa Riente, stone plaque.

II. Social Sets

Social History - Family, Faith & Club

"The Beach Club is the limelight for the privileged; at midseason there are 2,000 people in Palm Beach, all wealthy, but only 150 can be seated for dinner at The Beach Club. That is society." - The New York Times, 1915.

"Palm Beach is a resort without a top or a bottom. No one ever really knows where they stand when the sky is the limit. Palm Beach is not predicated on the principle that men are free and equal but that they are privileged and unprivileged." - The New York Times, 1916.

The story of Palm Beach's social life, its adjective-filled accounts of comings-and-goings, ins-and-outs, galas-and-gowns, is customarily told by glossy photographs, superficial images of sparkling bold-faced names engaged in halcyon pleasures unrestrained by means or consequence. But rather than this publicized view of private lives, the resort's social saga may be more appropriately told as a representative history, however incomplete and imperfect its timeline. It needs to be a multi-dimensional narrative, chronicled primarily by its long-standing family circles, churches, and clubs. With today's Palm Beach serving as a backdrop for a vast calendar

(Left) Top: The Dimick family's Cocoanut Grove House hotel was one of the island's social hubs before Henry Flagler transformed Palm Beach into a resort. *(Library of Congress)*

(Left) Bottom: The Royal Poinciana Hotel, The Breakers and the Whitehall Hotel became popular social gathering spots. *(Library of Congress)*

of charitable fundraising events, it would be misguided and mistaken to necessarily consider the current groundswell of naming rights donations, guest lists, centerpieces, and menus as components of Palm Beach's actual social history.

When Cleveland Amory wrote, "Palm Beach may not have been among the first resorts but it certainly is among the last," he may have meant Palm Beach is predominately made up of people who live somewhere else, where everyone is someone somewhere, distinguished for something. Newport and Bar Harbor were firmly identified with the accepted social establishment, but Palm Beach became the ultimate winter destination to indulge in the guilt-free excesses they might be reluctant to show-off in their own hometowns. As early as 1910, "Social leaders from all major cities headed tables in the Royal Poinciana's dining room." Today's Palm Beach is no longer, as it was once described, "a migratory crowd that flits in and out for a few days stay," or "a playground for millionaires in the heart of the jungle," or "a cosmopolitan assemblage of expected visitors of a certain class who loll in lazy luxury".

Palm Beach is actually a social conglomerate, made up of New York's Fifth Avenue, Boston's North Shore, Philadelphia's Main Line, Pittsburgh's Sewickley, Chicago's Lake Forest, and Detroit's Grosse Pointe. It has become predominately a residential enclave with much the same class structure found in Tuxedo Park or Chestnut Hill. Where most resorts, even today's Newport and Bar Harbor, are based on an economy that thrives on attracting tourists, Palm Beach exists primarily on deflecting outsiders, its commercial venues expected to be town-serving. Ironically, these are the same social expectations that visitors fled from a century ago when they crossed the railroad bridge seeking Palm Beach as a haven for high-living.

"Old regimes valued names above notoriety and lineage over bank book." The Social Ladder, May King Van Rennselear and F. F. Van De Water. New York: Henry Holt & Company, 1924.

The Making of Society

"Women brought society to America; they did not originate a social system in America. They transplanted one from wherever they came, Holland, England, France. It was nurtured by them here and has always been peculiarly their sphere." The Social Ladder

At the end of the Civil War and with the emergence of The Gilded Age, brownstones turned into marble mansions. A highly-visible wealthy social class chose to model itself from European aristocracy, complete with Louis-Louis architectural styles, top hats, and Worth gowns; everything except royal titles. These conspicuous elements formed a codified hierarchal society for the new fortunes made in finance, railroads, and industrialization.

The August Belmonts were among the first to roll out an actual red carpet to welcome guests and introduce gourmet dinner as something more than meatloaf and peas. Sizable private mansion dining rooms and ballrooms adorned with John Singer Sergeant portraits accommodated soirees and quadrilles once held at Delmonico's or Sherry's. Robber barons by day became philanthropic black-tie swells at night. Gentlemen smoked cigars, hunted at Thomasville plantations, golfed in Newport, and built houses in Tuxedo Park. Women played cards, worried about etiquette, wore gloves, and made up guest lists.

While in an earlier era, newspapers relied on illustrations, the introduction of cameras allowed for the mass production of images. At the time, there was no social class that enjoyed being photographed more than the opulently-dress Vanderbilts and Belmonts.

(Left) Top: The Royal Ponciana Hotel stationery.

The *Social Register* was first published in 1887. It began as a list of names culled from calling cards belonging to New York's exclusive Fifth Avenue denizens, cotillion dance invitees, National Horse Show patrons and Metropolitan Opera box holders.

America's pearls-and-white-gloves flock grew from within rather than from without. As social circles flourished from generation to generation, it created a widening impenetrable gap, more of a wall, between them and the rest of the world, the dressmakers, booteries, glove makers, chefs, and butlers. Fifth Avenue mansions and country estates in Lenox became story-book settings. High society was perceived as a Mt. Everest, something to climb. Any harsh criticism of gluttonous greed was usually smoothed over by philanthropic contributions to social causes and cultural institutions.

Cottage & Hotel Life

"Mrs. Astor's society is based on publicity, showiness and, the dreaded word, striving… Ours is based on family and the quiet enjoyment of the people we love," not the flashy and the conspicuous." The Social Ladder.

Before Henry Flagler's auspicious arrival in 1894, the Lake Worth colony's seasonal social life consisted of simple unsophisticated gatherings called "at homes." Held at one of the lakeside cottages, among them, Reve d'Ete, Fleur d'Eau, or at Primavera, these "at homes" consisted of teas, picnics, houseboat and sailing parties, classic readings, and musicales. Victorian parlors weren't decorated by New York designers but rather carpets, china, silverware, and portraits were brought from their Northern homes. Its fifty-room Cocoanut Grove Hotel was known more for its convenience than offering luxurious amenities. Palm Beach was a place to get away from it all, not a gathering place to fret over dance cards and speak to social columnists.

In between church festivals and celebrations, the ladies formed a Fortnightly Club. The club's meetings were held in each other's living rooms where usually an evening supper was followed by song, piano poems, and literary readings. Sherry was served on the front porch. And, if they were fortunate, Anselme Robert sang while Belle Dimick played the piano. The Cottage Colony's men

(Right) Top: The Bath and Tennis Club opened for two seasons at the south end of The Breakers beach before their new facility formally opened in 1928 adjacent to Mar-a-Lago. *(Historical Society of Palm Beach County)*

(Right) Bottom: The Phipps family introduced polo at Phipps Field in Gulf Stream.

TO PREPARE SPORTS CENTER FOR SEASON

Phipps' Project, Town of Gulf Stream, New Sports Center

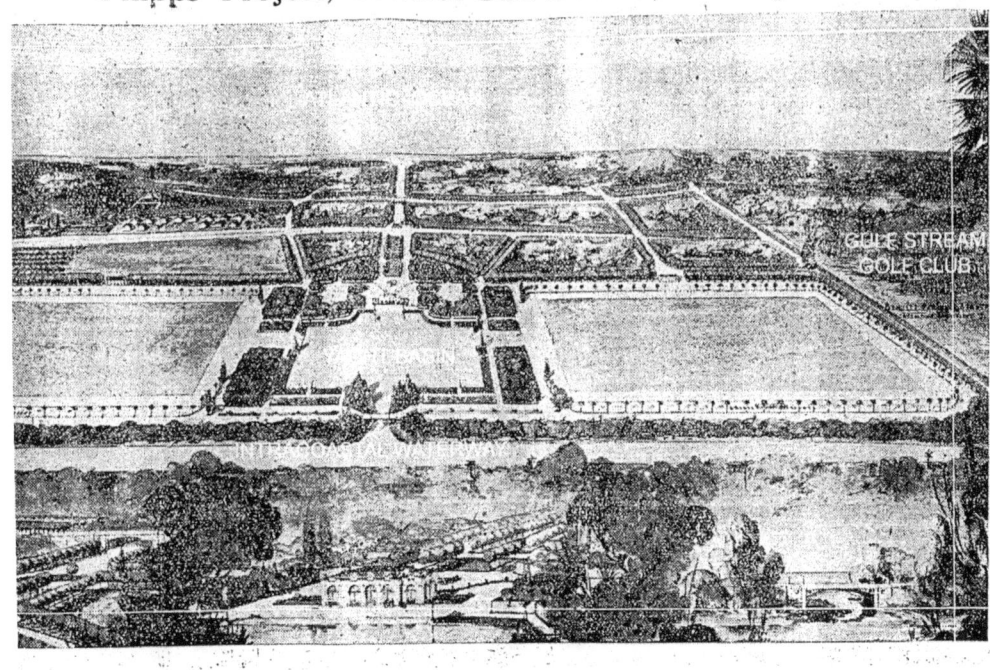

POLO FIELDS TO BE NUCLEUS COSTLY LAYOU[T]

Tennis Courts, Bridle Pat[hs] Will Be Built at Gulf Stream

Construction of a sports cente[r] believed to be the most magni[fi]cent in the state, on which $580,857 already has been spent for i[m]provement, is nearly complete[d] and will be ready for use this wi[n]ter, according to E. H. Currie, [of] the Palm Beach company.

The money is being spent in th[e] name of the Phipps estate. T[he] site is at Gulf Stream, betwe[en] Boynton and Delray on the Ocea[n] boulevard.

Two huge polo fields, a pra[c]tice field, tennis courts and brid[le] paths, all flanked by rows of tre[es] and hedges, may be seen when th[e] construction is finished.

Already the polo fields are i[n] shape for play and the grass o[n] them is cut every other day. Fir[st] games will begin some time in D[e]cember, when star poloists from a[ll] parts of the country will com[e] here.

The polo fields are 900 feet [in] length and 450 feet wide, flanke[d] on each of the sides by a safet[y] zone 30 feet in width, back o[f] which is a parking zone for auto[]mobiles. The practice field is 75[0] by 275 feet. The three fields ar[e] covered with the finest turf it [is] possible to grow in this locality[.]

Many Palms

(Left): Philadelphia grand dame Eva Stotesbury was considered among the town's social leaders. *(Palm Beach Life)*

(Right) Top: The Washington Birthday Ball signaled the end of the Palm Beach social season. *(Library of Congress)*

(Right) Bottom: The Charles Munn family. Left to right, Peter Pulitzer, Patsy Pulitzer, Charles Amory, Jr., Grace Amory, Gladys Munn Pulitzer, Reginald Boardman, Dennie Boardman, Carrie Louise Munn Boardman, Fernanda Wanamaker Munn, Gurnee Munn, Jr., Gurnee Munn, Sr., Frances Munn, Mary Munn, Charles Munn, Jr., Pauline Munn, Charles A. Munn, Sr., and, seated center, Charles Munn's uncle Noel Spenser Munn. *(Courtesy Anthony Baker Collection)*

organized sporting clubs. Charles Clarke formed the Palm Beach Yacht Club. Former Cleveland resident Charles William Bingham started the Pelican Island Yacht Club.

"Palm Beach is fantastically rich, idle, and gay—and useless." Harpers, 1915.

Henry Flagler's hotels introduced resort life on Lake Worth. In addition, Flagler should be credited for introducing the first cottage-as-showplace on the lake. Before Flagler built Whitehall, Palm Beach's own Taj Mahal, as a wedding present for his third wife, islanders were content with shingle-style and vernacular cottages. Thus, from then on, Palm Beach get-togethers moved from parlors to hotel piazzas and mansion ballrooms. Visitors who once came to fish and sail, appreciating Palm Beach's remoteness, now found themselves surrounded by tennis courts and golf courses. The sounds from flights of ducks and gulls were muted by orchestras playing from The Breakers porch or cakewalks in the Cocoanut Grove at the Royal Poinciana Hotel.

As more of the socially ambitious were drawn to Palm Beach as their destination, St. Augustine faded, becoming a mere whistle stop compared to the allure of Palm Beach. The hotels' daily program published an hour-by-hour schedule for golf, bathing, tea, concerts, dining, dancing, and even, lights out at ten. While some travel writers were enamored, "We are an imitative people, patterned after Monte Carlo;" others suggested, "Palm Beach is but a paper-maché Riviera."

Whether at The Breakers casino or Casa Bendita's loggia, from the Gilded Age to the Jazz Age, Palm Beach became an ever shifting stage set. Flagler's hotels succeeded in placing the wealthy and their daily extravagance on display, much like daily theater. As Palm Beach became known as a "camp ground for millionaires," everyone who had ever made a fortune, whether from Jell-O or Kleenex, gravitated to the island where displaying one's wealth was expected. And no matter the marathon of golf rounds, tennis sets, and pigeon shooting, social acceptance was Palm Beach's most sought after sport.

But after World War II, Palm Beach's resort world declined. Once composed of more than thirty Midtown apartment houses and twenty-eight hotels, by the mid-1960s the welcome mat had all but vanished, supplanted for the most part by condominiums and coop apartments with screening committees. Having lost its sense of hospitality for off-island visitors, today's social calendar is made up predominantly of publicized charity benefits and private "no pictures please" events held at home or one of remaining private clubs. Yesterday's taste for all-night parties has seemingly been replaced by civic altruism and philanthropic endeavors. Nonetheless, Palm Beach's social history, much like every other community, is portrayed by its focus on family, church, and club.

Family

"Society, first of all, is family; its primary meaning at present is fortune. Years ago, it stood for breeding; now it represents self-advertisement. Old regimes valued names above notoriety and lineage over bank book." The Social Ladder.

For more than a century, family life, often based on complex relationships engendered by multiple marriages, has played an enduring role in Palm Beach's social history. Among them, the

(Left): The Phipps clan at Gulf Stream.

Munn family's confluence of kinship generated a social class as tightly knotted as the Windsors. Today's Social Register does not list the Charles Munn name but the family's descendants form one of Palm Beach's formidable lineages. Among the names on the Munn family tree: Amory, Armour, Astor, Baker, Boardman, Bostwick, Dow, Drexel, Gurnee, Orr, Pulitzer, Ryan, Spreckels, Vanderbilt, Van Rensselaer, Wanamaker, and Waterbury.

Faith

What began in the late 1880s as the faith of four settlers in the "little red schoolhouse" along the North Lake Trail evolved into one of South Florida's oldest enduring religious community. The Episcopal Church of Bethesda-by-the-Sea has survived more than a century of storms and changes. And it has managed to retain one of its earliest buildings along the North Lake Trail, now a provate residence, as well as one of the island's most significant landmarks and community centers at the corner of South County Road and Barton Avenue.

Inspired by Florida's founding by Spanish explorers, the church's Gothic aesthetic is as apropos of 13th-century medieval Europe. Planned as "a little Spanish church set in a grove of coconut palms a hundred yards from the sea," The Episcopal Church of Bethesda by-the-Sea symbolizes "the nobility and aspiration of the soul, the mystery of Christian worship and the sense of the eminence of the Divine." The New York architectural firm of Hiss & Weekes is credited with the church building's cast-stone design, inspired as much by northwest Spain as the domestic architectural style of Ralph Adams Cram, the nation's most influential church designer.

Begun in 1897, the multi-denominational Royal Poinciana Chapel was established next to the Royal Poinciana Hotel as a place for hotel guests to worship or perhaps ask forgiveness for the previous evening at Bradley's Beach Club. It later moved and underwent renovations and additions, but the chapel has never lost its sense of pioneering purpose.

While the seasonal Catholic community began by worshipping at St. Ann's across the lake in West Palm Beach, St. Edward Church was built on the island in the 1920s. Much the same precedent was also experienced by the Jewish community. Jewish guests at the Royal Poinciana

(Right) Top: The boardwalk, casino and the beach cabanas at The Breakers were once at the center of Palm Beach's social life.

(Right) Bottom: The Fanjul family. *(Palm Beach Daily News)*

What began as the faith of four settlers in the "little red schoolhouse" along the North Lake Trail, evolved into Palm Beach's oldest enduring religious community

Hotel worshipped in West Palm Beach, even hosting fundraisers for the building of Temple Beth Israel in 1924. Eventually, after having services at the Bethesda-by-the-Sea Church, Temple Emanu-El moved to its own sanctuary on Sunrise Avenue before building its own synagogue on North County Road in 1974. Since then, other Jewish congregations have formed. At the Paramount Theatre, a non-denominational Christian church has occupied the space vacated by the movie theater since 1994.

Club

There was probably a time when nearly every Palm Beach resident, year-round and seasonal, was a member of a social or sporting club. Townspeople belonged to fraternal social clubs and church groups, and had year-round access to recreational activities. In Palm Beach for only an eight-week season and accustomed to the ready entrée private clubs offered at home, visitors replicated in Palm Beach the same social hierarchy they enjoyed up North. There was a time when wags described the Everglades Club as exclusive as Grand Central Station.

And certainly, when Paris Singer changed the name and the expectation of his hospital from the Touchstone Convalescents Club to the social and sporting Everglades Club, much like Henry Flagler before him, he had a strategic blueprint to transform and lead Palm Beach's society. Singer's club cuisine had to unseat Bradley's Beach Club. His orchestra had to be more entertaining than Bradley's table games. His commercial buildings needed to overshadow the Fashion Beaux Arts promenade along North Lake Trail.

With society architect Addison Mizner as his creative partner, Mizner was president of Singer's Ocean and Lake Realty Company, and Clarence Jones as the club's first president, the Everglades

(Left) Top Left: The Episcopal Church of Bethesda-by-the-Sea, façade.

(Left) Top Right: St. Edward Catholic Church interior.

(Left) Middle Left : Located on the North Lake Trail, the Episcopal Church of Bethesda by-the-Sea was the scene of church picnics, teas, and bazaars before it moved during the 1920s to its Barton Avenue location.

(Left) Middle Right: St. Edward Catholic Church, 144 North County Road. Some believe the name Edward represents Col. E. R. Bradley who was one of the church's most generous founders.

(Left) Bottom: Palm Beach Synagogue, 120 North County Road. Established in 1994, the orthodox synagogue met in the basement at Temple Emanu-El before, five years later, it acquired the historic Gothic-style building as its permanent house of worship.

Club was a success. The Beach Club's manager, Thomas "Tip" Reese, became the Everglades Club's first treasurer. Until the club incorporated in 1924, memberships were extended each season personally by Singer. With real estate to sell and the ever-growing need for investors, Singer published the names of new members. Soon, everyone wanted to get in.

But the Everglades Club was not the only club in Palm Beach. Guests at Whitehall and the Alba-Biltmore Hotel had the use of the Palm Beach Country Club and the Sun and Surf Club. In Midtown, nearly every hotel or apartment house had its own private beach area. Gus' Bath offered

(Left) Top: President Hugh Dillman, left, emcees a barn dance at one of the Everglades Club's theme parties. *(Palm Beach Daily News)*

(Right) Top Left: Hugh Dillman, president of the Everglades Club. A former actor, real estate agent and social secretary, Mr. Dillman's second wife was Anna Dodge. When Mr. Dillman retired, the club allowed him to buy the Paris Singer house on Via Parigi. *(Palm Beach Daily News)*

(Right) Top Right: Everglades Club, staircase. *(Library of Congress)*

(Right) Bottom: Everglades Club, Worth Avenue façade and porte cochere entrance.

memberships in the Palm Beach Swimming Club. The Palm Beach Athletic Club, the Coral Beach Club and the Seaspray Beach Club each had several hundred members.

The popularity of these clubs caused members needing more exclusivity to form other clubs. To the south, the Gulf Stream Golf Club and the Bath and Tennis Club were organized. Until there new Joseph Urban-designed facility opened in late 1927, the B&T had encamped at the south end of The Breakers beach. North of Palm Beach, avid golfers formed the Seminole Golf Club. Along with an abundance of private clubs, Palm Beach was brimming with European-style night clubs. The Patio, Montmartre and Colony Club were Café Society's favorites.

Today's activities at The Mar-a-Lago Club closely resemble the same social profile that the Everglades and the B&T maintained for more than sixty years. The Mar-a-Lago Club stages concerts, galas, luncheons, and charity balls attended by its members, their guests and others who pay to attend, much as the Everglades Club did for more than fifty years. The Everglades and

(Left) Top: Bath and Tennis Club. Lunch on the beach at the B&T, *l. to r.*: Jim Blair, Alastair Mackintosh, Ellen Frazer, Burks Carstairs, Mabel Cochran, the fiancé of the gentleman to her right, Prince Hohenlohe. *(Lucius Ordway Frazer Collection)*

(Left) Bottom: Sun and Surf Club, Sunrise Avenue at North Ocean Boulevard. *(Historical Society of Palm Beach County)*

Top: Louwana, view from the pool-tennis house east toward the main house. The Gurnee and Marie-Louise Wanamaker Munn house was the scene for numerous house parties. Charles Munn's house, Amado, was next door.

the B&T, as does the Palm Beach Country Club, preserves an enforced blackout, an inter-phasic reality where members are not permitted to speak about or publicize any club activities. Thus, there are several thousand Palm Beach residents whose social life is no longer recorded as part of Palm Beach's social history. The old social order is not extinct but simply no longer in public view.

Palm Beach's social life no longer rises-and-falls on the like-mindedness of a private club dictated by the ins-and-outs of a lone social arbiter, a Paris Singer, Marjorie Merriweather Post, or Eva Stotesbury. Today's *Social Register*, as published by Forbes, overlooks imperfect marriages and familial flaws, once its gold standard. Instead, the *Social Register* showcases a more fluid social order where the Old Guard, who have not gone completely into hiding, and New Money share the same pages, if not the same tee times or tennis courts.

Each generation revises and alters its perception of society. In contrast to the days when everyone belonged to the same club or church, Palm Beach offers multi-level dimensions, a social Rubik's Cube where everyone is equally regarded as the top of the heap.

(Left) Top Left: Wally Findlay with two of Palm Beach's most notable social leaders, Mary Sanford and Rose Kennedy.

(Left) Top Right: Having become a popular Palm Beach personality as manager of the Sun & Surf Club, after World War II Jack Mitchell opened the Coral Beach Club.

(Left) Bottom: Mar-a-Lago, an after party following the Everglades Club Costume Ball. *(Palm Beach Life)*

Valentine's Day Children's Party, Royal Poinciana Hotel, 1925. *(Palm Beach Life)*

Everglades Club Costume Ball, 1927. *(Palm Beach Life)*

The Guggenheims spent winters in Palm Beach with other Our Crowd families — the Warburgs, Schiffs, Lewisohns, Loebs and Seligmans.

Jewish Society in Old Palm Beach

"Radiogram for Mr. Baruch." "Mr. Seligman, your guests have arrived."
"Telephone call for Mr. Goldwyn." "Mr. Kaufman, your table is ready."
"Mr. Gershwin is at the center table in the Orange Gardens."

These are probably the last names you would expect to hear from behind the walls of Palm Beach's Everglades Club or the Bath & Tennis Club. But, during an earlier era, Palm Beach was once a far more complex social mosaic. Prominent Jewish families were among the town's largest property owners, played an active role in the commercial community, and were members and guests at the town's most exclusive private clubs. Today, the town's residential areas reflect a diverse mix, but clubs such as the Palm Beach Country Club have lost their earlier, more inclusive ambience that once made them representative of the resort's unrivaled standing among the world's social vanguard.

(Left) Top Left: Jules Bache. *(Library of Congress)*

(Left) Top Right: In 1926, Irving Berlin married the socially prominent Ellin Mackay. Mr. and Mrs. Berlin were frequent guests at the Everglades Club. *(Library of Congress)*

(Left) Bottom: Otto Kahn, second from left, at Oheka I with, left to right, Jane Sanford, his daughter Margaret (Mrs. John Barry Ryan), Betty Bonstetten, Nancy Yuille, and Maurice Fatio. A founding member of the Bath and Tennis Club, Kahn was a popular social figure in Palm Beach. *(Lucius Ordway Frazer Collection)*

Instead, for the past fifty years, these three clubs have been too often the controversial focal point for defining the fellowship between Christians and Jews. This mindset has been molded as much from cryptic lore and legend as actual reality between equally exclusive social circles whose shared past is as common as it is conflicting. Despite today's more progressive social dynamic, these tightly-knit enclaves remain the resort's most coveted invitations while the make-up of their membership remains the crux of the protracted rift between the resort's Nobs and Swells.

From the beginning, Gilded Age Knickerbockers were joined by members of New York's aristocratic Jewish community at Henry Flagler's St. Augustine and Palm Beach hotels, bringing with them their own social chain of command. Significant Jewish personalities have been overlooked in the recounting of Palm Beach's social history, where the same familiar discriminating history has been repeated so often everyone believes it.

Palm Beach's social jungle

Ever since Henry Flagler left his Standard Oil office at 26 Broadway and transformed Florida's East Coast into the American Riviera, New York and Palm Beach have shared the same social caste. While Palm Beach's carefree ambience may have appeared to be an escape for Gilded Age old-money millionaires, newly-minted merchants, and Our Crowd's fashionable financiers, they did bring with them their inflexible cast-iron social chain of command. Palm Beach's social inner sanctum was always reserved for the few whether they were part of a Jewish or WASP clique.

Palm Beach's earliest social circles revolved around bridge parties and luncheons at the Royal Poinciana Hotel, afternoon tango teas at The Breakers, bird shoots at the Palm Beach Gun Club, houseboat gatherings on Lake Worth, and dawn-to-dusk gambling at Bradley's Beach Club.

Located in the town's jungle-like North End, where the Palm Beach Country Club was eventually built, by 1903 the Gun Club's roster registered sixty members, culled predominately from existing members of New York's gun clubs. At Col. E. R. Bradley's Beach Club, membership was limited to non-residents of Florida and, most likely, handpicked by Bradley's discerning stamp of approval. When the Beach Club opened its Bradley's Floral Park Casino, Bradley invited only one hundred and fifty guests — Vanderbilts, Astors, and Fitzgeralds among them. This was during an era when more than three thousand guests attended the season's social highlight, the Washington Birthday Ball at the Royal Poinciana Hotel.

Even so, the well-heeled Jewish winter colony's social history was never documented or detailed with the same boldfaced stature as the island's more ubiquitous social leaders, whose entertainments had filled Newport and Saratoga social pages. Their history has been marginalized, often revised to appear anomalous, depriving Palm Beach of a multi-cultural past that established it as a unique international resort. This is in contrast to Newport's and Long Branch's staid regional appeal, the Hamptons' uncompromising country-club crowd, and Bar Harbor's unchanging quaintness.

Our Crowd in Palm Beach

In 1905, tin magnate Meyer Guggenheim's death at a lakeside Palm Beach house made worldwide headlines. The Guggenheims spent winters in Palm Beach with other Our Crowd families — the Warburgs, Schiffs, Lewisohns, Loebs and Seligmans. They were later joined by Paleys, Annenbergs, Ittlesons and Gimbels, among others, as well as Jewish political, film and theater celebrities. There were times when prominent Jews shared the same tennis courts and golf courses with Palm Beach's prevailing social sets as well as moments when they were subject to the similar patterns of exclusion, discrimination and quotas practiced in every other club, university and city in the United States.

After the Civil War and into the 20th century, the United States was an anti-Semitic society where Jews experienced an arbitrary exclusion that was never codified.

Our Crowd, and the wealthy Jewish social strata that came after them, acquired enormous fortunes, intermarried with the fervor of their blueblood counterparts, night-clubbed on County Road, and dined on Worth Avenue. Palm Beach's seasonal private clubs accepted Jewish members only later to reportedly rule them out; then, include them. Club memberships were as unpredictable and arcane as inclusion in the Blue Book.

The 1923 *Social Register* listed Henry Seligman, Jules Bache, Otto Kahn, Louis G. Kaufman and Bernard Baruch; Felix Warburg and Mortimer Loeb Schiff were omitted. In the 1929 edition, Adolph Lewisohn and Mortimer Schiff were listed but the Warburgs were still excluded. Moreover, the guest registers and membership lists at Palm Beach's hotels and private clubs, most notably The Breakers, Everglades Club, Bath & Tennis Club, and the Palm Beach Country Club, evolved in several distinct, if not episodic, stages. The available archival records document a more complex social mosaic of Palm Beach when prominent Jewish families were guests at its hotels and club members.

From the late 1890s until the 1960s, the *Palm Beach Daily News* and *The New York Times* reported almost daily on Palm Beach's social events and guest lists, providing a detailed who's who, when members of Our Crowd were social insiders. *The New York Times* archive has amassed more than fifteen hundred detailed who-was-with-whom stories from inside the Everglades Club. And considering the number of private clubs, nearly everyone in Palm Beach was a member of a social club. Then, during the 1970s, a period after the Palm Beach Country Club became predominately Jewish, the Everglades Club, the B&T, and to the same degree, the Palm Beach Country Club, closed their books, forbid press coverage, and withdrew from the public eye. Since the enforced blackout, *The New York* Times has reported on only two club events.

Club events were no longer publicized; membership rosters were closely held, often publicly acknowledged only in a member's obituary. In 1960 the Everglades Club announced that "only club events that are member-sponsored and private parties will be permitted without being publicized." The club "could no longer obstruct traffic and have events where guests outnumbered members and appear to be commercial activities."

And today, while only a small percentage of the town's residents belong to the town's Big Three — Everglades, Palm Beach Country Club and the B&T — for many, the world within the private clubs remains the only sport in town.

Grand hotels

In 1877, when the Joseph Seligmans arrived in Saratoga for their tenth season at the Grand Union Hotel, they were intercepted by a clerk who announced: "Mr. Seligman, I am required to inform you we have instructions that no Israelites shall be permitted in the future to stop at this hotel." That confrontation ignited a national controversy, the nation's second "Battle of Saratoga," as media pundits called it.

The selective exclusion of Jews from several resort hotels began a series of prominent investigations and editorials decrying the practice. At the time, hotels were free to discriminate without any legal recriminations and the practice continued. In the case of the Grand Union, the owners responded with a smokescreen of objections, complaints by women guests and proclaiming that "Hebrews like the Nathans and the Hendricks (Sephardic Jews socially established in New York) were always welcome" but "not the ostentatious class, the Seligman Jews" (German Jewish arrivistes) whose presence was blamed for ruining resorts. And yet, in 1884 at Long Branch, an Ocean Avenue casino and club with a ballroom and reading room, included among its founding patrons the Henry Seligmans, the Maurice Sternbergers and A. J. Drexel.

Fifty years later, Mr. and Mrs. Adolph Simon Ochs celebrated their fiftieth wedding anniversary in February 1933 at The Breakers in Palm Beach with a family dinner for twenty-five in the hotel's dining room. Ochs, the publisher of *The New York Times*, and his family were seasonal visitors at The Breakers, as were other A-list Jewish families who stayed at the hotel ever since Flagler's first oceanfront hotel opened as the Palm Beach Inn at the turn of the century. A decade earlier, these same families made the Hotel Ponce de Leon, Flagler's Old Florida resort in St. Augustine, their seasonal retreat.

Yet, as much as Ochs and his circle enjoyed swimming at the Breakers Casino and gambling at Bradley's Beach Club, they probably realized that for every Jewish guest who stayed at The Breakers, there were others, perhaps less prominent, whose reservations were repeatedly refused and would stay nearby at the Royal Poinciana, Whitehall, Alba, or later, The Colony.

From the inception of Flagler's hotels, newspapers recorded the guest lists, which included the names of Jewish guests. In 1920, Samuel and Goldie Paley hosted a dinner for three hundred at the Alba Hotel. The Jerome Kerns entertained the Fatios and the Amorys aboard their yacht, Showboat. Sophie Loeb spent her winter sojourns at The Breakers. In 1931, Felix Warburg celebrated his sixtieth birthday by playing golf at The Breakers. "The Warburgs arrive ..." read the headline the following season, as Felix and Frieda Warburg registered at The Breakers with their family, Mrs. Jacob Schiff, Mrs. Gerald Warburg, Mrs. Walter Rothschild and Frederick Warburg. Eventually, the Warburgs purchased a house on Eden Road on the island's North End. Mrs. Warburg passed her winters playing bridge and canasta with neighboring Our Crowd families, the Stroocks, Nathans and Lewisohns.

Although it is still widely believed hotels imposed selective quotas for Jewish guests, Jewish guests and entertainers were welcomed at Palm Beach hotels operated by Jewish owners. The Alba and Whitehall hotels were favored among Hollywood stars and studio czars, including Samuel Goldwyn, Edgar Selwyn, Lee Shubert, and Marcus Loew. At the Alba, Adolph Zukor hosted a dinner for New York Mayor James J. Walker following a tea at Sailing Baruch's hotel apartment.

Developed by H. M. Heckscher, The Alba opened in February 1926 only to close and reopen shortly thereafter as the Ambassador Hotel, part of the national chain. Subsequently, the hotel was owned by New York real estate titan, S. W. Straus. After acquiring an ocean front estate on Sunrise Avenue, Straus built cabanas and converted it into the Sun-and-Surf Beach Club for his hotel guests.

In 1942, hotel magnate A. M. "Sonny" Sonnabend purchased the Ambassador, which became known as the Biltmore Hotel, the Whitehall Hotel, the Sun and Surf Beach Club, and the Palm Beach Country Club. An active member of the American Jewish Committee, Sonnabend, whose holdings later formed the Sonesta hotel chain, also launched the Chart House in Annapolis, Maryland as a place for Jewish travelers to spend the night when driving between Boston and the South.

The ten-story Martin Hampton-designed Whitehall Hotel became a choice destination for many of Palm Beach's Jewish visitors. As Sammy Eisen's orchestra played in the hotel's Jardin Royal, well-known New Yorkers, Mosette Morganstern, Mrs. Harry Schwartz, Irving Geist and Issac Levy joined Seventh Avenue and Wall Street personalities, according to articles in *Palm Beach Life* magazine during the 1930s and 1940s.

And although there is no public record of discrimination at any Palm Beach hotel, in March 1965 the Anti-Defamation League of B'nai Brith (ADL) picked The Breakers for its first test of the Civil Rights Act, asking the Department of Justice to bar the hotel's practice of discrimination.

The ADL sent written reservation requests, some with Jewish and non-Jewish sounding names; those sounding Jewish were denied reservations while those with Protestant-sounding names were accepted. The Breakers at first denied the charges but months later the hotel agreed to abide by the civil rights discriminatory policy. Press reports during and after the incident stated that The Breakers had never permitted Jewish guests even though it was the favored hotel of the Our Crowd set whose visits had been publicized for more than forty years. Social registers published during the 1920s had even listed Frederick Lewisohn's winter address as, The Breakers, Palm Beach.

A longtime seasonal guest at The Breakers, ADL board member Samuel Untermyer was a founder of the "Browning Club," an informal group of prominent New Yorkers who gathered at The Breakers casino. A celebrated New York corporate attorney and prominent international Jewish rights advocate, Untermyer was also one of Palm Beach's largest property owners. In 1916, he purchased a thirty-two-acre ocean-to-lake property for $75,000 adjacent to the newly opened Palm Beach Country Club by the Flagler-based Florida East Coast Hotel Company. After his wife's death, Untermyer sold the property for $775,000 to Mark Rafalsky, a Manhattan real estate developer, who subdivided the parcel into a subdivision known today as the Rafalsky Tract. It includes the Beach Club and Ocean Lane, in addition to the following streets: Country Club, Fairview, Ridgeview, North Lake Way, Hi-Mount and Slope Trail.

(Left) Top Left: Samuel Untermyer. *(Library of Congress)*

(Left) Top Right: S. W. Strauss. *(Library of Congress)*

As Palm Beach's popularity grew and hotels became more crowded, resort life became more exclusive. Seasonal visitors emulated Bar Harbor and Newport's cottage colony, moving their social networking from hotel rotundas to private clubs and into their own private terraces and loggias.

Club rules

The Palm Beach season was brief and its social Brahmins did not want to share sporting facilities with local, year-round residents who had their own private clubs and recreational resources. Thus, private clubs for tennis, golf, swimming and entertainment were organized.

In January 1919, Paris Singer opened the Everglades Club with three hundred and five members, subsequently limiting membership to five hundred. Several years later, The Bath and Tennis Club opened with cabanas and tennis courts on a stretch of oceanfront south of The Breakers beach. Then, in 1927, E. F. Hutton and Anthony J. Biddle syndicated the B&T with two hundred members and built a new $1 million complex that would rival Newport's finest beach club. Designed by Joseph Urban on South Ocean Boulevard, the club was sited across from the Hutton's own seasonal retreat, Mar-a-Lago.

Initially, both clubs shared the same rule book and much the same memberships, rooted in the extended families found in the *Social Register*, Philadelphia's Main Line, Boston's North Shore, New York's private dining clubs, and Long Island's beach and golf clubs. While the clubs alternated the same officers and boards for many years, the B&T's membership was more diverse and international than the more inflexible Singer-directed Everglades Club.

From their inception, the Everglades Club and the B&T held widely-publicized private and public functions, fashion shows, gala charity fundraisers, musicales and political luncheons. Their popularity led to more clubs: the Seminole Golf Club, the Oasis Club and the Gulf Stream Golf Club.

According to available records, for many years the Everglades Club welcomed Jewish guests to its luncheons, teas and dinners, mostly those who were also members at the B&T. The club's popular tombola fashion shows were attended by ladies and their guests. At the Woolworth Donahue's supper dance, Jules Bache was a guest along with the John Jacob Astors and the Alfred Vanderbilts. In February 1929, Mr. and Mrs. John Bryden held a luncheon in the Orange Gardens for Mr. and Mrs. Henry Seligman. When the Seligman's grand-daughter visited Palm Beach, *The New York Times* reported, "Miss van Heukelom, one of the prettiest young girls to visit Palm Beach, has been entertained with dinners and teas at the Everglades Club." The Henry Seligmans hosted the luncheon in honor of Metropolitan Opera diva Maria Jeritza when she opened the Everglades Club's concert series for The Society of Four Arts.

Showman Flo Ziegfeld and his wife, actress Billie Burke, were houseguests of the Gurnee Munns and the E. F. Huttons before becoming seasonal residents and members of the Bath & Tennis Club. In March 1933, when the Everglades Club presented Josef Kallini, tenor, the event's patrons included Eva Stotesbury and Esther Paley, wife of Jacob Paley, a 20th Century Fox studio executive and brother of Samuel Paley. In February 1940, Capt. Alistair Mackintosh hosted a dinner before the club's popular backgammon night with the Munns, Guests and Frederick Lewisohn. Charles Loehmann, the discount clothier whose mother, Frieda, founded the national department store chain in her Bronx kitchen, was an Everglades Club member until his death in 1986.

The island's largest galas, Red Cross, Heart and Good Samaritan Hospital fundraising events, were held at the Everglades Club for decades. More than nine hundred fifty guests attended the 1965 Flamingo Ball, with the Orange Gardens aglow with pink and white lights, including Estée Lauder, Bernard and Alva Gimbel and Enid Haupt.

When the Everglades Club faced foreclosure, banker Louis G. Kaufman, the son of Jewish immigrants, was among the club's few members who secured the club's future. President of New York's largest bank, Chatham-Phoenix National Bank, Kaufman had served as finance chairman for General Motors for more than twenty years.

For many years, the Everglades Club rule book's Section XIII stated that no member may "introduce as a guest or bring upon the premises any person when such person might essentially believed not to be acceptable as a member." Guests were limited to five visits to the club during the season while there were another set of guidelines for caregivers, house guests and golf guests. To become a member, according to the club's rule book, an individual must already be a member of a "leading club in the place of his residence." Once the prospect obtained three letters from current Board of Governors, one of whom could not be the club's president, and three letters from members, the name would be posted for a period of two weeks allowing for members to comment on the membership. At that time, a prospective member could be blackballed with two negative votes.

Fifty years after Joseph Seligman was turned away from Saratoga's Grand Union Hotel, his nephew Henry Seligman became a member of Palm Beach's Bath and Tennis Club. In February 1929, the Henry Seligmans and their party of eighteen guests attended the B&T's formal opening of the new Urban-designed facilities, as did Jules Bache, who entertained a party of twelve family and friends. Mr. and Mrs. Edward F. Hutton shared their table with the Bernard Baruchs. Baruch, whose wife was Episcopalian and father was Meyer Guggenheim's doctor, was a lifelong friend of E. F. Hutton's, mentioned prominently in Hutton's obituary as one of the major influences in his life. The Mortimer Loeb Schiffs were also among the opening dinner-dance crowd. In 1935-36 Samuel Goldwyn, the Hollywood film producer, was regarded as one of the B&T's favored guests. By 1973, the B&T listed seven hundred members and declared it a "family club," allowing only one public benefit annually and ruling that members could propose no more than two prospective applications per year.

Following the B&T's opening, Anthony Biddle and E. F. Hutton headed a group that opened the Oasis Club, located at one of E. R. Bradley's tennis buildings remodeled into a club by Joseph Urban. Organized as a "men only" club, the Oasis Club was a place to transact business, play cards, have dinners and stage boxing matches, usually following a tea dance. The Oasis Club's opening beefsteak dinner and dance was held in February 1929, hosted by the club's vice president and treasurer, Jules Bache.

What made the Oasis Club unique was its membership mix. Bluebloods, Vanderbilt, Hutton, Doubleday and Conde Nast, among them, were joined by Bache, Kahn, and Schiff, among other Jewish residents. Interestingly, the roster also included several local, year-round townspeople, which was highly unusual. Although the Oasis Club did not last through the Depression years, it began one of Palm Beach's lasting social legacies, the exclusive Coconuts, founded by the resort's single men to give an end-of-season party to repay social obligations.

Established at The Breakers in 1914 as the Fishing Club, the Sailfish Club of Florida is regarded as the oldest private club in Palm Beach, having moved to its present North Lake Way site in 1932. Several years ago when the Sailfish Club was notified by the State of Florida that its membership selection process was discriminatory, the club adapted the following credo: "The

(Left): Hollywood movie executive and Wells Road resident Nate Spingold. *(Library of Congress)*

Board of Governors of the Club shall not consider race, color, religion, sex, national origin, age, handicap or marital status of the applicant, applicant's spouse or applicant's family." Reportedly, the club does have minority members. In his memoir, *The World I Lived In*, entertainer George Jessel, "Toastmaster General of the United States," writes about his fishing trips with Woolworth Donahue and his membership in the Sailfish Club during the 1930s.

The Palm Beach Country Club was built in 1916 by Flagler's Florida East Coast Company on the old Gun Club's extensive ocean front for the exclusive use of hotel guests at the Royal Poinciana Hotel and The Breakers. It quickly became one of the resort's most popular social and sporting venues. Along with the Peabodys, Whitneys, Huttons and the Sanfords, Samuel Untermeyer and Harry Rosenfeld were among the first to tee off on the Donald Ross-designed golf course. It became the setting for some of the state's most notable golf tournaments. For more than a decade, Rube Goldberg hosted the annual New York artist and writer's golf tournament at the Palm Beach Country Club, a week-long event that included receptions at the Everglades Club and the Royal Poinciana Hotel.

In 1952, A. C. Sonnabend sold the Palm Beach Country Club to an investment group for $1 million. After an extensive makeover, the club reopened the following year with Morris Brown as its first president and Edward Cohen, Edward Goldstein, Harry Fine and Louis Leibovit serving on its first board. Today the Palm Beach Country Club is one of Palm Beach's most exclusive clubs, with Nelson Peltz, Charles Bronfman and A. Alfred Taubman among its members, and governed by many of the same membership rules as the Everglades Club and the B&T, although it emphasizes a member's philanthropic donations.

The Mar-a-Lago Club, established in 1995, offers an array of amenities and allows publicized events, closely resembling the same social profile the Everglades and the B&T maintained for more than sixty years before they became averse to any public acknowledgment of club events. As the Everglades and the B&T continue to preserve their enforced blackout on all the club's social activities, The Mar-a-Lago Club stages musical concerts, galas, luncheons, and charity balls attended by its members, their guests and others who pay to attend charitable fundraisers.

The development of exclusive clubs in Palm Beach paralleled the shift of Palm Beach's social realm from hotel lounges and European-styled nightclubs to parties and dinners in private homes as the resort's seasonal guests became permanent residents with their own tap rooms and ballrooms, including the island's prominent Jewish families who were a part of the island's A-list social set.

Top Left: Rube Goldberg and family. As head of the New York Artists and Writers group that visited Palm Beach every winter, Goldberg was a popular addition to events at the Everglades Club and Palm Beach Country Club. *(Library of Congress)*

Top Center: Bernard Baruch. A close lifelong friend of E. F. Hutton's, Baruch was a member of the Bath and Tennis Club and was seated at the Huttons' table for the club's opening. *(Library of Congress)*

Top Right : Alva and Bernard Gimbel. Involved in Palm Beach's charitable gatherings, the Gimbels' ocean-to-lake estate was located at 1435 South Ocean Boulevard. *(Library of Congress)*

Above Left: Whitehall Hotel, advertisement. The Whitehall was always a popular hotel with Jewish guests. *(Palm Beach Daily News)*

Above Right: George Jessel. Jessel and his wife, Norma Talmadge, owned a house in the South End during the 1930s. *(Library of Congress)*

At home in Palm Beach

Palm Beach houses have a mythical aura. Ever since Otto Kahn entertained Ned and Eva Stotesbury in 1917 at his first oceanfront house, known as Oheka I, Palm Beach's Jewish families have been some of the resorts most prominent homeowners.

In 1920, after visiting Palm Beach for several seasons, the Henry Seligmans purchased a lot on Sunset Avenue next door to local banker T.T. "Tommy" Reese. Referred to as the "American Rothschilds" in Stephen Birmingham's book, *Our Crowd: The Great Jewish Families of New York*, the Seligmans commissioned architect Marion Sims Wyeth to design Casa Mia. The Seligman's hosted the New York String Quartet Ensemble and Metropolitan Opera baritones in their music room, "a room of noble proportions," as invitations were accepted the island's A-list — Huttons, Singers, Stotesbury, Cluetts and Vanderbilts. Mrs. Seligman's teas introduced progressive international personalities, hosting Mme. Halide Edib, author and feminist leader of Turkey.

In January 1928, when New York's Cardinal Patrick Hayes visited Palm Beach, Casa Mia was the setting for the prelate's welcome dinner attended by the same smart set that were aboard Harrison Williams's yacht the next day and at the luncheon for the Cardinal at the B&T. Following the Seligman's death in March 1935, Casa Mia was sold by Gurnee Munn's real estate agency, Munn, Hull & Boardman, to Joseph Schenck, president of United Artists and Alfred C "Blumey" Blumenthal, a Fox Theatres executive, who managed Florenz Ziegfeld's theatrical interests. In announcing the sale, Munn said the producers would make the resort their winter residence.

A few blocks north of the Seligmans, Nate and Frances Spingold purchased Las Puertas, a Spanish-styled house on Wells Road. A movie studio executive and champion bridge player, Nate Spingold, and his wife, Frances, a New York couturier known as Mademoiselle Frances, hired Addison Mizner, and later, Treanor and Fatio, to design their winter retreat. Mizner transformed the Spingolds' living room into a forty-two-by-eighteen-foot drawing room and added a new loggia with a high vaulted ceiling and tiled floor, a grill room with Gothic vaults and stained-glass medieval windows, enhancing the dining room with XVIth-century panels from the Cathedral of Pamplona. With interiors designed by Valentine, Inc., a second-floor Louis XVI master bedroom suite was created with French blue-and-rose marble. When the Spingolds purchased the property to the east for their swimming pool with salt water piped from the ocean, an exterior flying staircase was added that joined the poolside terraces with their second-floor master bedroom suite. The

> Dr. WILLIAM YOHANNAN SAYAD
> Palm Beach Res.: Brazilian Court Hotel.
> Phone 2-3191.
> Palm Beach, Florida.
> Permanent Res.:
> Colleges: Davidson, '17; Yale, '21.
>
> Mr. and Mrs. MORTIMER SCHIFF (Adele G. Neustadt)
> Palm Beach Res.: "Eleda," South Ocean Blvd.
> Phone 2-3171.
> Permanent Res.: 932 Fifth Ave., New York City.
> Clubs: New York Yacht, Piping Rock, Lotos, Grolier, Army and Navy, City, Midday, National Golf, The Pilgrims, National Arts, Bath and Tennis, Oasis, Florida Embassy.
> Yacht: "Dolphin."
> College: Amherst, '96.
> Adult: Mr. John Schiff.

Spingolds' pool became a popular spot for Hollywood stars such as Norma Talmadge and Joan Crawford to bask in the Palm Beach sun.

Farther north on County Road, Otto Khan, regarded as the "King of New York," built Oheka III, a twenty-three-room Renaissance oceanfront palace designed Treanor and Fatio. In 1928, Khan's daughter, Margaret, married John Barry Ryan, Jr., grandson of financier Thomas Fortune Ryan, known as the richest man in the world. One of the most significant arts patrons, Kahn supported the Russian Ballet, the Metropolitan Opera, playwright Eugene O'Neil, as well as the renovation of the Parthenon.

In Midtown at 160 Barton Avenue, Jules Bache's winter cottage, La Colmena, was an Addison Mizner design. Its distinctive forty-five-foot living room is all that remains of the original, as it is now referred to as "The Ballroom House." Bache purchased the house from the Angier B. Duke estate following Duke's death in 1923. Bache's clients included J. D. Rockefeller, Edward Harriman and Jay Gould. His eclectic Palm Beach houseguests included Jefferson Davis Cohen, the English godson of the Confederate president, whose French racing stables were considered among the world's best, earning Bache and Cohen hand-delivered invitations to be among the

Top: Mr. and Mrs. Mortimer Schiff. *(Social Register)*

Widener's inner circle at Hialeah. A resident for more than thirty years, Jules Bache died in Palm Beach in 1944, leaving his immense art collection to the Metropolitan Museum.

In the South End estate district, New York attorney Louis S. Levy and his wife, the former Norma Rabinowitz, bought El Solano at 720 South Ocean Blvd. from Harold Vanderbilt. A half-mile south of the Levys, Kuhn, Loeb scion, Mortimer L. Schiff, and his wife, Adele, built one of Palm Beach's most unique houses, Casa Eleda, designed Treanor and Fatio.

While the economic upheavals of the 1930s reversed the fortunes of some of Our Crowd's gilded Palm Beach lives, others persevered and eventually made Palm Beach their home during the 1950s. After the war, new North End subdivisions were carved from the Boom era's ocean-to-lake estates where, even though reportedly some restrictive covenants forbid Jews from ownership, Palm Beach continued to attract the nation's Jewish patrician class. Felix Lilienthal, Max Horwitz, the Albert Zifferblatts, A. A. Goldbergs, Nathan Yamins and the Herman Rothbergs are some of the New York families who built seasonal cottages in the town's Midtown and North End.

At 1465 South Ocean Boulevard, the Bernard Gimbels settled on an ocean-to-lake property that was later subdivided. The ocean side is now entertainer Rod Stewart's house. Every winter Alva Gimbel would board the Silver Meteor with her Dalmatian, Chieftain, and make the trip to Palm Beach. The Gimbels were often seen at Hialeah race track, guests of their neighbor, Joseph Widener. The Gimbels owned Sak's Fifth Avenue when the department store's Worth Avenue venue became the first branch outside of New York.

The Annenberg sisters, Janet Hooker, Evelyn Hall and Enid Haupt, were among Palm Beach's most benevolent residents who also lived in Newport and New York. In Palm Beach, Janet Hooker lived at Il Palmetto, the Fatio-designed Widener residence, recently renovated by Netscape founder, Jim Clark. After meeting ambassadors during the Red Cross Ball in Palm Beach, she became one of the nation's largest contributors to renovating U.S. State Department buildings; her gifts to the Smithsonian included the Janet Hooker Hall of Gems, Geology and Minerals. Her sister, Enid Haupt, purchased a house on El Dorado, site of the Palm Beach Garden Club's house and garden tour in 1961. In a newspaper interview, Haupt credited architect Philip Johnson with influencing her design decisions with the house, especially its expansive windows and door openings. The

(Right): Goldie and Samuel Paley. The Paleys were longtime Palm Beach residents, first visiting during the 1920s. *(Palm Beach Daily News)*

Enid Haupt Conservatory at New York's Botanical Gardens is considered one of the grandest spaces in the world. She sold the house in 1971 to her sister, Evelyn, who was a significant arts patron, a major Museum of Modern Art benefactor.

Samuel and Goldie Paley made Palm Beach their winter home for more than a half century. Following her husband's death, Goldie Paley donated the funds for the Samuel Paley Pavilion at the Rehabilitation Center for Children and Adults on Royal Palm Way. Mrs. Paley traveled to Palm Beach with her staff in a private jet provided by her son, William Paley, CBS founder and president, who was also a part of the Palm Beach scene.

Beginning in the 1930s, and for the next four decades, Henry Ittleson, and his wife, Blanche, made Palm Beach their seasonal retreat. Founder of C.I.T. Financial Corporation, Ittleson was regarded as the innovator of revolving credit accounts. Blanche Ittleson built a unique Japanese-inspired temple-style house and gardens in 1956 at 756 Slope Trail. It was designed by Howard Major.

Palm Beach today

Just as yesterday's four hundred has become today's four thousand, Our Crowd's once social elite has evolved. Jewish residents are no longer the few but half the town's population. The island now has several synagogues and the Palm Beach Fellowship of Christians & Jews formed in 1993, an organization promoting fellowship among religions and cultures. The organization focused on intolerance, anti-Semitism and discrimination.

Gone are the days when private clubs dictated the town's social standards. Today's more consequential social whirl is concentrated on philanthropic and charitable causes. Outsiders become insiders by their generosity, not genes. However, remembering the camaraderie and the spirit that once existed between the Old Guard and Our Crowd serves as a reminder when there was nowhere else in the world like Palm Beach.

(Left) Top: Casa Eleda, entrance surround. Treanor & Fatio, architect. Among Palm Beach's most popular couples, Mortimer and Adele Schiff were founding members of the Bath and Tennis Club.

(Left) Bottom: Blanche Ittleson *(Palm Beach Daily News)*

TO THE GLORY OF GOD
AND IN COMMEMORATION OF
· MARY CLUETT MULFORD ·
WHO ON JAN·22·1889 ORGANIZED THE WOMANS' GUILD OF
· THE CHURCH OF BETHESDA BY THE SEA ·
THE FIRST CHURCH SOCIETY TO BE FORMED IN PALM BEACH
· CHARTER MEMBERS ·

DORINDA HALE BRELSFORD	ETTA ELMIRA HENDRICKSON
LAURA BELL BRELSFORD	EMILY CADBY HENRY
MARY C BRELSFORD	MARY BRELSFORD HOOD
AMANDA ROCKWELL CLUETT	ELIZABETH MARSH KINZEL
NELLIE A CLUETT	JEANIE E MADDOCK
HELEN FRANCES CRAGIN	ELIZABETH G MATTHAMS
ELLA J DIMICK	EMILY WILLING PENDLETON
ALICE GOSS DUN DOUGLASS	MARSENA NELSON ROBERT
IDA MAY REED HAIGHT	VICTORIA ADELAIDE ROOT

ELIZABETH M WORTHINGTON

Frances Payne Bingham.

Women of Worth

"Palm Beach is a woman's idea of paradise, bosoms, pearls, necklaces and diamonds. Everything is done furioso, double forte, big pearls, big diamonds and big jewelry. After dinner, imagine four hundred women gathered, each one determined to slay the others, with a pang of envy at the beauty of her attire ... It's a Coney Island in silks and satins"

— National Courier, 1916.

From its inception, Palm Beach's seasonable convergence of debs, divorcées, dowagers, and grande dames established the resort's unrivaled supremacy among the world's feminocratic fiefdoms. Yet, despite a rich history of remarkable accomplished women known for their pioneering and groundbreaking achievements, time and again these same ladies are recognized for the size of their fortunes, husbands, or fashion sense. No matter the litany of selfless deeds, their charitable philanthropic endeavors have always been considered less important than the weight of their diamonds.

(Left) Top: Women's Guild of The Episcopal Church of Bethesda-by-the-Sea. The first First Ladies of Palm Beach.

(Left) Bottom Left: Frances Payne Bingham Bolton. The Cleveland native completed the congressional term of her late husband Chester C. Bolton before being elected for fourteen terms to the House of Representatives. She championed equal rights for women and desegregation. In 1952, her son Oliver Bolton joined her in the House of Representatives. In 2000, a documentary film was produced about her life, *Reaching out for Liberty and Light: The Life of Frances Payne Bolton. (Historical Society of Palm Beach County)*

(Left) Bottom Right: Lucy Lacoste Maddock. A prominent literary figure, Maddock would swim from the Palm Beach pier to The Breakers pier. The Parisian-born Lucie Maddock, a poet, novelist, playwright and radio personality, became known as much for being a suffragette in the women's rights movement as her British-born conservative husband had been recognized for his contributions to the building of Palm Beach. *(Courtesy of Maddock Family)*

Unlike idyllic retreats having made a name by offering therapeutic mineral baths or magical spring water, a season in Palm Beach was known to heal the loneliness of a tycoon's daughter and the melancholy of widowdom. "Heiress weds hotel clerk," read a national newspaper story with a Palm Beach dateline after a Midwest widow with a newly inherited fortune left Palm Beach with more than just a souvenir following a three-week courtship. In her 1922 novel, *Fantine Avenel*, author Lucie Lacoste has her protagonist imagine Palm Beach as a "... a vision, surpassing a dream" where she will finally be able to "wear a well-cut bathing suit."

Even though women were the town's leading social, cultural, and philanthropic pillars and held a considerable economic presence, owning many of the town's fashionable shops, they were still subject to ignoble stereotypes. Palm Beach was a refuge for gold diggers lurking in beach cabanas, fortune hunters stalking the Jungle Trail, and spoiled self-centered poor little rich girls secluding themselves in suites at The Breakers.

These frivolous labels continued long after the women's suffrage movement won the right to vote in 1920. At the Club de Montmartre, theatrical impresario Florenz Ziegfeld was staging Palm Beach Nights with a flock of chorus girls. For Palm Beach, Ziegfeld proclaimed, "the day of the beautiful but dumb girl is over." He assured residents the women dancing at the Royal Palm Way club were supervised by a live-in matron and their performances would be "dignified ... no flimsy bathing suits but suits that reach the knees and limbs completely covered by stockings."

Building alliances

Established in 1889, the Woman's Guild of The Episcopal Church of Bethesda-by-the-Sea was the first church society formed on Palm Beach. The selfless group, including Amanda Rockwell Cluett, Frances Cragin, Ella Dimick and Jeanie Maddock, hosted some of the island's earliest charitable and cultural benefits.

(Right): Lucy Lacoste Maddock and her son, Paul Maddock. In 1909, Lucy Maddock's husband Sidney was described as Palm Beach's most interesting person; by 1918, he was regarded among the town's wealthiest. The entrepreneur transformed nearby farmland into the successful Palm Beach Pinery, a sizable plantation that shipped pineapples from Palm Beach to London. Along with his considerable speculative lake and oceanfront properties, Maddock built the Olympic and Dixie movie theaters, as well as several Clematis Street commercial ventures in West Palm Beach. *(Courtesy Maddock family)*

Leading Palm Beach suffragettes Amy Phipps Guest and Lucy Lacoste Maddock were joined by Katherine Duer Mackay, wife of communications magnate Clarence Mackay. As president of the Equal Franchise Society, Katherine Mackay spoke out on the need for "women of all classes to work for civic improvement through the agency of the ballot box" for more than a decade before the 19th Amendment was ratified in August 1920.

During the 1920s, the Women's Civic Club of Palm Beach led cleanup drives, pressed for sidewalks along County Road, opposed lighting along Ocean Boulevard, and advocated the establishment of a North End fire station.

Among The Garden Club of Palm Beach's first accomplishments after it was organized in 1928 was formulating an aesthetic and functional plan for the town. The club's president, Marion Wallace Rappeleye McKinlock, did much to transplant the City Beautiful Movement to Palm Beach, retaining Chicago-based Bennett, Parsons and Frost to formulate the seminal plan. Although only a few of the firm's actual recommendations were ever fully realized, the plan led to the creation of the town's first planning commission, where three Garden Club members served on the first board.

Whatever Palm Beach's outward conservatism, it did not impede unflinching Palm Beach women from advancing progressive social causes. In 1935, the *Social Index* declared Anne Shaffer Phipps the first woman bestowed with the accolade "Social Immortal." Shrouded in the mystique of Old Money, Mrs. Henry Carnegie Phipps joined the resort's exclusive pantheon that included Henry Flagler, Paris Singer, Addison Mizner, Henry Bemis and The Rev. George Morgan Ward. On an island where many secure a place in eternity by their philanthropy, Mrs. Phipps surpassed the cottage colony's well-intentioned by fashioning her own guiding principles.

Mrs. Phipps not only wrote a check but she also took an active role in an organization's decision-making, whether building a conservatory in Pittsburgh, establishing an agricultural college in India, or endowing the first organization in the United States to focus on a single disease, the Phipps

(Right) Top: Isabel Dodge Sloane. *(Lucius Ordway Frazer Collection)*

(Right) Bottom Left: Rose Kennedy. *(Palm Beach Life)*

(Right) Bottom Right: Mary Sanford. *(Lucius Ordway Frazer Collection)*

Institute for TB research and treatment. And later, as the sole beneficiary of her husband's estate, she continued the charitable work they had begun together: health care for the less fortunate, public parks, inner-city model garden apartments for working families, civilized care for the mentally ill, and family planning. She lobbied for legislation requiring physicians to dispense information about birth control.

Keeping with her mother's tradition, Amy Phipps Guest sponsored Amelia Earhart's first transatlantic flight in 1928 and lent her Palm Beach estate, Villa Artemis, as a convalescent home for sailors during the war. She traveled solo on a private peace mission in 1956 to the Mideast, meeting with President Nasser and Prime Minister Ben-Gurion.

In 1938, the Town of Palm Beach honored Ella J. Dimick, independently of her late husband, Elisha N. Dimick, with "a scroll lettered on parchment" designed by Treanor & Fatio, praising her as "a courageous example of pioneer womanhood" and for having "aided carving an empire out of a primitive jungle."

For her heroic service in the French Underground during World War II, Mary Astor Paul Munn Allez was awarded the French Legion of Honor and the American Medal of Freedom. She served as president of the American Aid Society in France. Under the code name Pauline, she risked her life to save others during the Nazi occupation when she "carried messages rolled in her stocking garter."

Long before Worth Avenue became one of the world's leading destinations for women designers and business moguls — and the Duchesse de Richelieu "forsaked her social career" to head an interior decoration firm — Palm Beach shopkeepers welcomed women as entrepreneurs on equal ground.

As early as 1910, The Breakers and the Royal Poinciana Hotel leased space to Mme. Najla Mogabgab, whose emporium offered "French novelties and Japanese goods." Mrs. Frohman's Exclusive Shop sold lingerie, spring hats and linen suits. Over on Main Street, Mrs. M.E. Roache advertised her famous homemade cakes.

(Left): Mary Sanford and Dame Celia Farris. *(Palm Beach Daily News)*

Opened in 1916 on North Lake Trail, the Fashion Beaux Arts shops established Palm Beach as an international fashion catwalk. Bonwit Teller and Cartier were joined by specialty shops from New York, London and Paris, including Alice Evrard, Sara Hadley, Lucile Ltd., the Lady Duff-Gordon and Miss L. Brogan.

Thus, a few years later when the Everglades Club opened a Worth Avenue shopping arcade, as well as venues along Via Mizner and Via Parigi, there was considerable interest in women-owned businesses having a Palm Beach address. Grace Hyde's hat shop was one of the first twenty shops proposed for Via Parigi. Mary Wanamaker Warburton opened a produce store on newly created Via Mizner, offering farm-fresh eggs and milk. Mrs. Franklin opened at 11 Via Mizner. Esthelle Lucas offered shawls at 256 Worth. They were soon joined by Bella Darling, Miss Marie Ballet, Madame Yovin, and Hattie Carnegie.

On Via Mizner during the early 1960s, Lilly Pulitzer unplugged her orange juicer and began selling colorful and comfortable shifts, called the Lilly Shift. Pulitzer's iconic barefoot designs transformed her into an international fashion legend alongside Lillie Rubin's more glamorous ball gown offerings.

Women of note

The year before the 19th Amendment was ratified, Ruby Edna Pierce became the editor and manager of the *Palm Beach Daily News* and *Palm Beach Life* magazine, a position she held for thirty-five years. Pierce was a founder of the St. Agnes Guild, an organization of young business women organized in 1935, as well as one of the original supporters of the United Way, when it was still known as the "Unified Drive." She had begun her career at fifteen, when the newspaper office was still owned by Henry Flagler and located at the Royal Poinciana Hotel. Pierce became "the dean of Florida's newspaper women."

Following her father's death in 1925, Bessie F. Fenn became the manager and resident pro at the Palm Beach Golf Club, situated between The Breakers and the Royal Poinciana Hotel. A *New York Times* headline read "Woman golfer rules in Palm Beach," as she was the only woman in the United States who had ever run a major country club course. One of the few women golf professionals in the United States, she ran the club for thirty-four years with three male assistants.

Grace Morrison pursued her passion for aviation while a secretary for the Treanor & Fatio architectural firm's Palm Beach office. When the Women's Aeronautical Association was established in 1932, Morrison became its first president. At first, the group was dedicated to advancing the role of women in aviation but soon took on the job of expanding the Palm Beach area's aviation facilities. The woman's group was the foundation for the Palm Beach County Airport Association, which also tapped Morrison as its president, determined to make the local airfield "one of the state's largest and best airports." Morrison led the fundraising efforts, including the 1934 Aviation Ball held at the Bath & Tennis Club. The following year, the PBCAA deeded four hundred forty-eight acres to the county, allowing it to become a regular stop for transcontinental passengers and mail. Following her death in 1936 in a traffic accident, the airport Morrison Field was named in her honor.

While Palm Beach children are often typecast, Barbara Hutton and Sue Whitmore both grew up in Palm Beach, sharing similar generous indulgent childhoods where having everything was the norm. And yet, their later lives were a startling contrast of values.

Top: Mona Williams, later Countess Bismarck. *(Lucius Ordway Frazer Collection)*

Bottom: Ailsa Mellon Bruce. *(Lucius Ordway Frazer Collection)*

Barbara Hutton's enchanted Palm Beach youth was a labyrinth of extravagance. On Golfview Road, she lived at Hogarcito where the Everglades Club golf course was her playground. When she played with her cousins, it was either at Mar-a-Lago or Cielito Lindo, two of Palm Beach's most fantastic playgrounds. At the age of five, she lost her mother and gained the fortune that for the next fifty years enabled her to have everything she wanted except the contentment she desired but never attained. For her celebrated New York debut, Rudy Vallee crooned with the Meyer Davis Orchestra in an other-worldly fantasy for what may have been the last blissful moments before her downward spiral of misfortune and heartbreak. Staged by the renowned Joseph Urban, Hutton greeted twelve hundred guests. She stood in a forest of silver birch trees with sprays of eucalyptus beneath ceilings covered in blue gauze and star lights with balconies banked with evergreens and poinsettias and tables covered with Persian mountain violets and countless Claudius roses.

But later, she was never able to recreate this imagined reality for herself, often racing to the altar only to spend her honeymoon in a hospital or sanitarium. Every melodramatic moment and movement of her life was recorded by newspapers and magazines, and forever captured by the flash of a camera. In the end, exiled in a Beverly Hills hotel room, without family, friends or fortune, lacking her health and mind, she died alone comforted by her jewelry and framed images of her family. Her splurges and perils became fodder for page-turning books and made-for-television movies.

Susie McRae Hopkins Whitmore's private railroad cars and fairy tale surroundings might have led her into a rudderless life without a sense of gravity, but instead she became one of Palm Beach's most revered social leaders. Recognizable for her tiaras and her scarves, her parents, Russell and Vera Siegrist Hopkins, maintained the nation's largest private zoo. At Veruselle, the Hopkins' eighty-eight-acre estate in Tarrytown, the family pets included a baby hippopotamus. The son of John Russell Hopkins, a wealthy Atlanta banker, Mr. Hopkins's elopement with the seventeen-year-old Vera Siegrist was a social scandal, as Mrs. Hopkins was heir to Dr. Joseph Lawrence's Listerine pharmaceutical fortune.

In Palm Beach, the Hopkins family owned the property north of the Palm Beach Country Club, where later, Addison Mizner's largest seaside castle, Playa Riente, was built. During the late 1920s, Mrs. Whitmore, along with her two sisters and brother, inherited equal shares of their mother's estate, valued at more than $7 million. Sue Whitmore made her debut in 1931, married in 1933, and in 1936, she commissioned architect John Volk to design her own first Palm Beach house, Twin Banyans on El Vedado Road. When Whitmore moved to her Worth Avenue villa in the 1950s, she did something unimaginable today — she invited the entire town to her housewarming.

Palm Beach's social establishment has always been made up of women who, either through family or marriage, were *of* Palm Beach. But there were also those who had no previous connections, and earned a life in Palm Beach. Among them were Estée Lauder, Yolande Fox, and Deedy Marix, the town's first woman mayor.

Back when Palm Beach was afloat between Camelot and Capri, as barefoot islanders twisted the night away, ga-ga over quiche, tail fins and turbans, luncheons and dinner dances were chaperoned by the likes of Mary, Betty, Brownie, Marjorie, Mary Lou, and Lilly. Elizabeth Arden and

(Left): Gloria Guinness. *(Lucius Ordway Frazer Collection)*

Much of Palm Beach's
social establishment has
always been made up
of women who,
either through family
or marriage,
were of Palm Beach.

Helena Rubenstein were counted on to make sure every flaw was concealed. And then, Josephine Esther "Estée" Lauder and her husband, Joseph Lauder, engraved Palm Beach on their already accomplished letterhead. Estée's Tell-a-Woman and Gift-with-Purchase campaigns had already given Madison Avenue a master class on the martial art of makeup marketing. Having made a name for themselves and become legends of their own making, the Lauders found themselves in a place where most everyone else had their places already made for them.

"Long before our lunches at Café L'Europe in Palm Beach, where it was always the best table, I first knew Estée in New York when I wrote for *The New York Times* and *Women's Wear* and she had a small retail shop," recalled Agnes Ash, former publisher and editor of the *Palm Beach Daily News* and *Palm Beach Life* magazine.

"She never stopped being hands-on. I recall at one of our Café L'Europe afternoons she was trying to come up with a name for one of her latest scents. It became Beautiful, I think. Over and over again, it was all she talked about, coming up with the right name," Ash said.

By the time the Lauders acquired the highly-visible oceanfront house at 126 South Ocean Boulevard in 1964, Estée was center stage, holding her own with rival Charles Revson. In the competitive elusive world of secretive crèmes and oils, you can never stop reinventing yourself, especially when your Prescriptives and Re-Nutriv bottles uncap the promise of eternal beauty, or at least for twelve hours under certain lighting. The Lauders' Clinique product line transformed over-the-counter cosmetics into clinical trial labs where white-coated shop clerks practiced the science of cosmetology. Long before today's needles, knives and lasers give women what Youth Dew could only promise, Estée Lauder's signature blue products could be found in the world's A-list ballrooms and bedrooms.

"She never stopped being a salesperson. If she could just touch the person, she thought she would always make a sale," Ash remembered. "Among Estée's many secret formulas had to be her secret for salesmanship, as when she was selling something, you sensed she actually believed what she was saying."

(Left) Top Left: Marjorie Merriweather Post. *(Palm Beach Daily News)*

(Left) Top Right: Sue Whitmore and Noreen Drexel. *(Palm Beach Daily News)*

(Left) Bottom Left: Ellen Glendinning Frazer. *(Lucius Ordway Frazer Collection)*

(Left) Bottom Right: Sue Whitmore and Dina Merrill. *(Palm Beach Daily News)*

And years later, one former Palm Beacher took exception with the public's perception of women as objects of beauty. In 1951, longtime Peruvian Avenue resident Yolande Betbeze Fox was crowned Miss America. Following her coronation, she balked at posing in a bathing suit, having graduated from a convent school and trained as an opera singer.

Fox's action caused the Miss America pageant to reassess its view of women, judging intelligence and physical beauty as comparable values. The pageant's sponsor, Catalina swimsuits, walked away, devising the Miss USA contest, where women were required to model bathing suits. "I'm an opera singer not a pin-up," said Fox at the time. Her Miss America tiara is now at the Smithsonian Institute.

In 1970, more than a half century since the town incorporated, Yvelyne "Deedy" Marix won a seat on the Town Council, becoming the first woman ever elected to a public office in Palm Beach.

"Because there were noticeable zoning changes, and my husband and I wanted to keep Palm Beach much the same way we had found it when we moved here in 1945, we thought one of us had to run for a seat on the Town Council," recalled Marix, who became council president in 1978. "And I suppose I was the one to do it.

"At first, no one took me seriously, maybe they thought I was a bit nuts. But then, I won."

In 1983, Marix became the town's first female mayor.

"Not everyone supported me, especially those who lost," Marix added. "Election night I recall overhearing someone say, 'The broad won.'

"Yes, she did," said Marix, who served five terms as mayor of Palm Beach.

Palm Beach women, constrained by fixed preconceived stereotypes for too many years, are today among the island's most dynamic individuals whose charisma and character resists any social mold.

(Right): Arnold Scaasi with Marylou Whitney and Eles Gilet. *(Palm Beach Daily News)*

BY-LAWS
OF THE
BEACH CLUB
INCORPORATED 1899

OFFICERS

E. R. BRADLEY, President

J. R. BRADLEY, Vice President

T. T. REESE, Secretary

ARTICLE I

Section 1. The organization shall be known as the "Beach Club."

Sec. 2. It shall be without capital stock.

Sec. 3. The object for which this Club is organized is for social purposes, including (as set forth in the Charter from the State) the privilege of conducting a private cafe, buffet, and such games of amusement as the management of the same and its members may from time to time agree upon.

High Rollers – Gambling on Palm Beach

"Our Palm Beach members want quick action and thrills, roulette and hazard. Card games are not thrilling." - The Beach Club, Palm Beach, 1913.

" ... Go to Palm Beach, which is not exclusive, but merry, sumptuous, expensive, and where there is a chance to meet many prominent men in the gambling rooms ..."
- Advice from a social arbiter when asked by a new millionaire how to enter the ranks of the *Social Register*.

The sky's-the-limit gambling at Bradley's Beach Club was already an internationally-recognized Palm Beach institution long before beach cabana bookies, trackside boxes at Hialeah's Jockey Club, and all-night escapades in Havana. The Beach Club's array of spinning wheels and tumbling dice made it the resort's most rapturous attraction. In between tea dances, cake walks and wheelchair rides, social swells were held spellbound by the sights and sounds within Bradley's gaming rooms.

In 1931, when James Paul Donahue died from an overdose during a card game in New York, tabloid headlines claimed Donahue had overstepped his allowance, drowning in gambling debts

(Left) Top: Without any known photographs depicting the Beach Club's interior, this drawing from a circa 1915 issue of a Pittsburgh newspaper is the only known representation of the activities within the private club.

(Left) Bottom: The official member's directory for The Beach Club. *(Historical Society of Palm Beach County)*

accumulated at "gambling haunts in Palm Beach." Hardly surprising news, as Palm Beachers once indulged openly in locker room card games, side-bet golf rounds and wagering on the boxing bouts at the old Oasis Club.

After Florida legalized horse racing in the early 1930s, Joseph Widener, along with several of his Palm Beach friends, were among the first to capitalize on pari-mutuel betting. In later years, when the island's Kenya Club bartender was arrested for running a bookmaking operation during the 1980s and a raid on a Worth Avenue gambling house netted twenty-seven arrests in 1997, residents most likely thought those nabbed deserved a place in Palm Beach's social pantheon next to Colonel E. R. Bradley rather than booked and fingerprinted at Palm Beach County Jail.

Bradley's Beach Club provided the ultimate fantasy in a town that had visitors stuffed with money and streets lined with imaginative picturesque houses, their facades more akin to stagecraft than any chapter of architectural history. The BC, as it was called, assured members and their guests an evening of unrecorded and undocumented pleasures experienced and known only to those there at the time, as shielded from outsiders and social historians as those activities pursued by today's private clubs.

Although the Beach Club generation has nearly vanished, Palm Beach has never lost its appeal as a place that exists outside of an accountable dimension, where unwritten rules dictate that money doesn't mean anything, but is the only thing that counts. For a select circle of players, it might have been the chance to make unbelievable payoffs; for others, it might have been the hypnotic spin and sport of the roulette wheel.

More than a half-century has passed since the blue blood's biggest bankrolls from 1898 until 1945 made the Beach Club the nation's most infamous casino. But gambling remains an influential part of Palm Beach's social history.

"My father once told me of a card game in a railroad car parked in front of the Royal Poinciana Hotel where $10,000 bought one chip." – Ector Munn.

"The real reason for the popularity of Palm Beach is not its climate or its hotels; it is Bradley's." -The New York World.

"The spin of the marble alone breaks the silence. When it falls, the croupier indicates the

winning number by pointing to the board, sweeping the chips, cash, paper IOUs into the drawer without a word." – The Pittsburgh Press, 1913.

In 1891, three years after Henry Flagler opened the Hotel Ponce de Leon in St. Augustine, Col. Edward R. Bradley and his brother John Bradley introduced casino-style gambling to Florida. The Bradleys moved their Club Bacchus dine-and-dice operation from Chicago to a cottage near Flagler's hotel.

In 1896, Col. Bradley, an honorary Kentucky colonel, was reported to be in Palm Beach scouting locations to establish a private dining-and-gaming club similar to his St. Augustine venue. Col. Bradley and his brother John, known as Jack, were fifty-fifty partners for their ventures in Chicago, New Orleans, New Jersey and Palm Beach, including hotels, restaurants, horses, race tracks, and private clubs.

In a short time, Bradley bought a lakeside cottage directly north of Flagler's Royal Poinciana Hotel, or the "Pounce-On-Em Hotel" as some locals called it. It became the island's most exclusive and popular diversion, giving Palm Beach a much-needed sophisticated cachet. With membership restricted to only out-of-state residents and offering haute French cuisine, Bradley's operational formula appears to have been modeled after Canfield's Casino in Saratoga, both establishments becoming widely-known during their time as the "Monte Carlo of America." Long before the Everglades Club, the B & T, and the Palm Beach Country Club were established, the Beach Club was society's preferred refuge.

Although gambling was illegal in Florida, The Beach Club's charter permitted it to conduct " … such games of amusement as the management of the same and its members may from time to time agree upon." The club was open for breakfast, lunch and dinner, allowing the gaming rooms to be open at all hours.

"People in Palm Beach do not play to win but for amusement because it is fashionable and not necessary. Here gaming is a pastime rather than a concern for money gains." – The Beach Club, 1913.

Nearly every season brought improvements to the club. A two-story octagonal gaming room was added, modeled after the Royal Poinciana Hotel's great salon. Chemin de fer and baccarat were added during the club's later years. Behind the main room's dimly-lit latticework, twenty

International Silver Solder Service, Black-Knight China, Full Kitchen Equipment, Bake Stove, Copper Kettles (sterling lined), Imported Glassware, Fine Oil Paintings, 1200 Yards of Imported Carpet (like new), Oriental Rugs, Mahogany Tables, Chairs, Furniture, Electrical Fixtures, Electric Radiators, Venetian Blinds, Dish-Washing Machines, Antique Hand-Painted Screens, Draperies, Linens, Hobart Mixing Machine, Coffee Urns, Ladders, Old Antique Brass Cuspidors, and Hundreds of Articles Too Numerous to Mention, in the World's Finest

BRADLEY BEACH CLUB

ATTENTION! DEALERS, HOTEL OWNERS and RESTAURANT KEEPERS:

Your Chance to Buy the Finest Equipment Available

AT YOUR PRICE

BRADLEY BEACH CLUB
ROYAL POINCIANA WAY
PALM BEACH, FLORIDA

Mr. S. Siegel, Auctioneer

armed and uniformed Pinkerton guards watched unobtrusively over the action at six roulette tables and two hazard tables.

In March 1915, Palm Beachers were "aflutter" when they awakened to read that Col. Bradley was arrested and the club was shut down. Although no gambling paraphernalia was found during the raid, a grand jury was convened to investigate a private investigator's allegation that Bradley's was one of the nation's largest gambling operations. None of the club's fifteen prominent "members" ever responded to subpoenas, including John "Honey Fitz" Fitzgerald, Rose Kennedy's father who was a close friend of the Bradley brothers. Shortly thereafter, "… the whirr of the roulette table, the rattle of chips and the voices from the dealers could once again be heard at Bradley's …"

Col. Bradley was known for keeping a loyal staff of about fifty men and twenty women who were housed within the Beach Club's compound. Married couples were not hired as they were believed to pass gossip among each other about the club's guests. The staff was paid only once at the end of every season. Of course, this did not include the customary regular cash envelopes paid to local and state politicians and law enforcement officials. Noted for his philanthropic endeavors in Kentucky and Palm Beach, Bradley was most generous to local Catholic and Jewish charities.

In 1947, an estate auction, a Palm Beach tradition, was held at Bradley's. Several years later the Beach Club was torn down, leaving only the vestige from Bradley's house and this plaque, commemorating one of Palm Beach's most unique landmarks. And while the roulette wheels and dice games may have vanished, Palm Beach still attracted the world's high rollers ready to gamble everything.

(Left) Top: Following Col. Bradley's death and his specific instructions that the club would be demolished and the land willed to the town for use as a park, an auction sale liquidated The Beach Club's fixtures.

(Left) Bottom: Aerial view of Beach Club. Col. Edward R. Bradley (inset) and his brother John Bradley presided over The Beach Club, pictured in this aerial overlooking the north wing of the Royal Poinciana Hotel. *(State Archives of Florida)*

OASIS CLUB IS FORMED BY MEN OF PALM BEACH

New Club Obtains Bradley Property on Main Street Near Ocean for Club Building

The Oasis Club

However much Palm Beach's private clubs can be notorious for their exclusivity, the one that defied most of the stereotypes usually associated with their selection process, surprisingly proved to be one of the cottage colony's most popular.

In 1914 Col. E. R. Bradley built a private sporting enclave north of The Breakers that would serve as lodging for a visiting British tennis team. But, because of World War I, the British squad never arrived and the amenity remained vacant. A decade later, a group of notable society men bought the property and turned the facility into an exclusive men's club, which was "sadly lacking in Palm Beach." It was a resort where bachelors and gentlemen could "play cards and discuss the affairs of state … without fear of interruption."

And thus, the legendary men-only Oasis Club was formed in 1926, led by Anthony J. Drexel Biddle Jr., who immediately hired his architect, Joseph Urban, to remodel the club into a more sophisticated social rendezvous for "the masculine element." While Urban was at work designing the Bath & Tennis Club, the E. F. Hutton new house and the Paramount Theater, he transformed the abandoned buildings located on the eastern end of Main Street into a Mediterranean showplace.

The renowned Viennese theatrical designer added a two-story wing with sixteen bedrooms, a large walled patio, a double staircase that led from the upper-level reception room onto the patio, and a fountain for the walled courtyard. The sizeable enclosed outdoor dining area was

(Left) Top: Oasis Club, newspaper headline. The Oasis Club was a gentleman's club. *(Palm Beach Daily News)*

(Left) Bottom: The Oasis Club, façade. *(Palm Beach Life)*

floored with pine needles, thus called Pine Needle Garden. Considered one of Palm Beach's most enchanting spaces from the moment it opened in January 1927, an Urbanesque mural in the grill room depicted a woman riding atop a camel being led by Arabs to a desert oasis.

Along with Biddle as president, the club's officers included W. Forbes Morgan and E. Clarence Jones as vice-presidents, and Jules S. Bache, treasurer. The founding membership included William K. Vanderbilt, Coleman DuPont, Otto Khan, E. F. Hutton, Clarence Geist, Henry Rogers, Mortimer Schiff, Paris Singer, Henry Seligman and Thomas Tipton "Tip" Reese. Much like the original Bath & Tennis Club, the Oasis Club had a diverse membership with its bachelor-members carefully screened to ensure their suitability for Palm Beach's debutantes and the "fair sex."

During this first season, women were permitted only on Friday afternoons for tea, leaving the men to pursue backgammon contests, card games and other masculine diversions. The following season, architect Maurice Fatio, who stayed at the club during his bachelor days, added another wing of bedrooms. It was then the club allowed women to join them for "tea dansants," where the Pine Needle Garden was the scene for boxing matches and beefsteak dinner dances. Between bouts, couples danced in the boxing ring to Dudley Doe's orchestra. Immensely popular, the matches were attended by as many as five hundred members and guests, becoming the type of "only-in-Palm Beach" entertainment that made the seasonal resort like nowhere else in the world. By the 1930 season, the Oasis Club had added Wednesday gala nights with a dinner-dance and performance by the Happy-Go-Lucky Boys.

However, the financial reversals of the 1930s caused the Oasis Club to shutter and the property reverted back to Col. Bradley, who had held a mortgage on the property. Before the club building was closed in 1937, the Civic Art Association of Palm Beach held several exhibitions at 147 East Main Street, as it was then known, using the facility's living-reading room area as a gallery space.

Institutum Divi Thomae

In 1940, Col. Bradley sold the club property for $40,000 to the Institutum Divi Thomae, a Catholic-sponsored scientific research organization founded five years earlier at the University of Cincinnati by the Archdiocese of Cincinnati and named in honor of St. Thomas Aquinas. Renamed Bradley Hall, the institute's mission, as set forth by Pope Pious XI's Pontiff Academy of Science in 1936, was to demonstrate there were no conflicts between its doctrines and scientific discoveries.

Having sold its patented irridation process for coffee roasting and foods, supposedly enriching them with Vitamin K, to General Foods, the institute launched its Palm Beach location as a center for the study of marine life. Under the leadership of biologist Dr. George Sperti, Archbishop John McNicholas and Monsignor Cletus A. Miller, a staff of twenty-five to thirty research associates and scientists conducted experiments in order to create medical remedies. In 1940, *Life* magazine published a headline that said, "Catholic Nuns turn Florida Beach Club into Marine Life Lab."

The Oasis Club's former bachelor quarters were converted into bedrooms for vesting nuns while another wing became laboratories. The bar was turned into a lab pharmacy, shelves once lined with wine and whiskey now held jars of sulphur and magnesium compounds. Nuns dressed in their habits seen kneeling on the beach north of The Breakers were not praying the rosary but were collecting seaweed to extract trace minerals for experiments.

(Left): The weekly boxing matches and beefsteak dinner dances made the Oasis Club one of Palm Beach's most popular venues. *(Palm Beach Life)*

According to the Institutum Divi Thomae beliefs, "biodynes" contained the key growth factors in cells. Thus, the holy sisters spent every season in Palm Beach extracting this essential cell matter from shark livers, chick embryos and kelp. Then, the resident scientists prepared various potential commercial remedies that, among other possible therapies, could control cancer. One of the institute's and Sperti Products Inc.'s most successful patents was for a "biodyne ointment" providing tissue respiration, the basis for Preparation H.

Later renamed the St. Thomas Institute, following World War II, the research group moved back to Cincinnati where it closed in 1987. In the ensuing years, the Palm Beach convent-style laboratory was dismantled and utilized by various organizations.

From club to cloister to condo cluster

By 1952, the complex had become housing for performers appearing at the Palm Beach Playhouse and members of the Apollo Boy's Choir. The choir's director, Coleman Cooper, had

attempted to house the entire choir at Il Palmetto, which he purchased at auction for $71,000 in 1950 when it was reportedly worth more than $2 million.

But neighbors complained, however angelic the prodigious child singers, and zoning officials demanded Cooper remove the fifty members of the choir from his six-acre residence. The young singers were moved to the Royal Poinciana Way facility. At that location, they were also able to perform using the expansive Urban-designed upper-level living area as a performance space. In addition, for several years during the mid-1950s, the American Society for the Aged, headed by Frank J. Hale, conducted seasonal seminars on the science and the philosophy of "the cell, the fundamental element of life."

Then, in January 1980, the original Bradley tennis club buildings and the adjacent 19th-century White Sands cottages were sold to a developer who paid $2.1 million for the three-acre oceanfront parcel. Plans called for the demolition of the sixteen existing buildings. Although some qualified for landmark status they were never designated, and they were replaced by a multi-story townhouse-condominium cluster complex.

Six months later, the facility's main building was gutted by an early morning fire deemed "of suspicious origins with no forced entry" by the Palm Beach Fire Department. The following month, salvage crews ripped out the fixtures and architectural details from all of the buildings. Subsequently, the town granted a demolition permit and plans for the development were approved.

Coconuts carry on club's legacy

Although the Oasis Club no longer exists, one of the customs that originally inspired the club's formation, the annual Coconuts party, is still celebrated by a select group of the town's gentlemen. Conceived in 1921 by the island's bachelors as an end-of-the-season madcap costume party to payback their hosts, beginning in 1956, the event was revived and reformed as a formal New Year's Eve celebration.

Left): Chris Dunphy drawing. Zito, artist. The annual end-of-season party given by Oasis Club members known as the Coconuts was revived during the 1950s. Transformed into a New Year's Eve black-tie event at Ta-boo, Chris Dunphy chaired the popular gathering for several years. *(Lucius Ordway Frazer Collection)*

1—Mr. and Mrs. Anthony J. Biddle. 2—Miss Marjorie Oelrichs. 3—Mrs. Malcolm Meacham. 4—Mrs. Harry Schaffer and Mrs. Russell Lo[...] [...]d Mrs. William J. Hyde, Mrs. Edward F. Hutton, and Mrs. Harris Hammond. 6—Misses Julia and Edna Brokaw. 7—Mr. and M[...] [...]fman. 8—Miss Genevieve Fox. 9—Maurice Fatio, James A. Blair, and the Misses Gertrude and Sarah Jane Sanford. At the Cocoa[...] [...] the Oasis Club.

—Photo by E. F. Foley

The first Coconuts parties were staged at the Palm Beach Country Club. They later moved to the Oasis Club where they earned the reputation as the resort's "wildest and fanciest" gatherings. After a dormant period during and after World War II, a group of seventeen "men of Palm Beach," including several of the original Coconuts, Christopher J. Dunphy, Milton "Doc" Holden, Caleb Bragg and Charles A. Munn, invited two hundred guests to join them in the Tangier Room at Ta-boo, where the popular custom was restarted.

Although Col. Edward R. Bradley's old tennis complex located on the east end of Royal Poinciana Way was demolished thirty years ago, its remarkable architectural and cultural history makes for a unique chronicle of past Palm Beach.

For nearly seventy years the versatile Main Street compound afforded a myriad of functions, ranging from a private men's club to a religious scientific research center that showcased the designs of the island's most renowned architects.

Yet, it was simply not enough to satisfy a more recent era's inclination to be modern.

When the picturesque ensemble of buildings was bulldozed in 1980 to accommodate the townhouse-condominium development, the loss was described by Charles Calhoun, a local columnist, as "… the sort of imposing buildings which in any other city might have been restored with great pride and publicity, and put to some contemporary use. But, not in Palm Beach where monumental architecture is more or less taken for granted."

Today, ninety years since the informal group's first soiree, the Coconuts' New Year's Eve party remains one of Palm Beach's premier occasions and a vestige from when the Oasis Club offered a unique departure from the resort's standard club fare.

(Left): Oasis Club's first Coconuts party, March 1927. *(Palm Beach Life)*

152

The Art Colony – Easels and Galleries

Long gone are the days when painters and sculptors added a sublime dimension to the art of living in Palm Beach when art galleries outnumbered real estate offices. But they are a reminder that resorts were intended as an escape from reality, rather than a mirror image of it.

And, as much as Worth Avenue's recent improvements complement the incomparable merchandise showcased within shop windows, they do not add the panache that the street's art gallery openings once created.

"It was unbelievably fabulous and fun. Everyone came and there were so many people, it practically blocked traffic," recalled Jimmy Barker, whose James Hunt Barker Gallery was a prime destination for nearly thirty years until it closed in 1998.

In 1954, there were three art galleries. By 1968, there were sixteen. Almost a decade later, the island's thirty-four galleries had positioned Palm Beach on the art world's radar west of Paris and south of Ogunquit.

But yesterday's Palm Beach was more than a congregation of collectors and openings. It was a place where artists came to live and work. Where better than Palm Beach to produce a recognizable style inspired by escapist fantasy?

(Left) Top: Loggia mural, Louwana. Zito, artist. One of Palm Beach's most colorful personalities, Zito was known not only for his caricatures but also his stylish loggia murals.

(Left) Bottom: The Breakers ceilings are detailed with artful murals.

Sketchbooks, easels and dark rooms

By the early 1900s, landscape easel painters and photographers were captivated by the newly-gilded resort's scruffy jungle trails and colossal banyan trees. Portrait artists were sought-after in between spins of Col. Bradley's roulette wheel and visits to the nearby ostrich farm.

Laura Woodward's studio overlooked the Hotel Royal Poinciana's lush gardens. Joseph J. Hollenbeck set up a studio-gallery in 1912. Hollenbeck kept studios at the Royal Poinciana Hotel, The Breakers and Whitehall before establishing a more extensive gallery and class space at 335 Worth Avenue. Pennsylvania artist Ben Austrian's landscapes became popular souvenirs. Austrian's studio was on Main Street across from the hotel where in 1918 he was joined by Edward Cooper, a prominent Newport photographer.

Cooper was soon joined by other society photographers. Also from Newport, E. H. Histed kept his wood dry-plate cameras and portrait lenses at his winter Worth Avenue studio. Chicago's William Louis Koehne had a photo studio designed within his Midtown oceanfront house Villa Zila, one of Palm Beach's earliest Modernist buildings.

Noted lensman F. E. "Frank "Geisler photographed Addison Mizner designed houses for an authoritative volume on the architect's work from the back of a pick-up truck driven around town by arts patron Alice Delamar. A former Wall Street banker who studied photography in Paris, Geisler arrived in Palm Beach in 1917 and lived at 256 Worth Avenue until his death in 1935. One of the era's pre-eminent artistic photographers, Geisler's work was shown at the Chicago Art Museum, Pennsylvania Art Museum and the Smithsonian.

After working with interior designer Paul Chalfin on Villa Vizcaya, Ohan Berberyan moved to Palm Beach in 1915. A few years later, he opened the Spanish Art Galleries across from the Everglades Club in partnership with Addison Mizner. Chalfin also moved to Palm Beach, keeping

(Left): Jimmy Barker surrounded by his two great passions, art and his Cavalier King Charles Spaniels, was a gallerist on Worth Avenue for more than four decades, first at Palm Beach Galleries; then, at his own James Hunt Barker Gallery. *(Palm Beach Daily News)*

an interior design studio aboard a houseboat docked on North Lake Trail in front of the Fashion Beaux Arts. Along with Mizner Industries, the Spanish Art Galleries provided paintings, sculptures, tapestries, plaques and carpets for the Everglades Club and almost every significant Palm Beach mansion built during the 1920s. A decade later, when Clarence Geist bought the Boca Raton Club, Geist retained Chalfin and Berberyan to furnish and accessorize the club's interior renovation.

The Mural at the Four Arts Library

Palm Beach can be described as an act of theatrical design. It was an artful tableaux staged for leisure pursuits, where Hollywood stars and Broadway legends once vacationed and double features and live performances at the Paramount and Royal Poinciana sold out. The life-size mural at The Society of Four Arts Library portico illustrates the resort's fascination for scenic illusion.

Renowned mural artist Albert Herter designed the library's mural in the entrance loggia. Herter, along with his wife, Adele, the distinguished Rockefeller-family portrait artist, were a Belle Époque couple who lived in Paris, New York and California. The Herters were East Hampton neighbors of Four Arts patron Mrs. Lorenzo Woodhouse. Adele Herter and Mrs. Woodhouse organized some of the earliest art exhibitions at the Four Arts. The Herter's East Hampton sixty-acre camp, The Creeks, is now best known as the summer hideaway of former Palm Beacher Ronald Perelman.

The mural's aesthetic presence is a formidable link to a page of international art history and a landmark reminder that Palm Beach is a great work of imagination. Albert Herter's paintings are at The Metropolitan Museum of Art, High Museum of Art and the Brooklyn Museum. His epic murals adorn Gare d'Este Paris train station, the National Academy of Sciences, the Los Angeles Public Library, and the St. Francis Hotel. He designed the world's largest drop curtain for the Denver Auditorium.

Albert Herter's father and uncle established Herter Brothers, the Gilded Age's most sought-after designers whose work smartened The White House and revamped Fifth Avenue mansions.

(Right) Top: Renowned portrait and mural artist Albert Herter created the mural at The Society of Four Arts Library in 1940.

(Right) Bottom: Gulf Stream Polo Mural, Turf Club. J. Clinton Shepherd, artist.

157

In 1959, the Herters' son, Christian Herter, was appointed Secretary of State under President Eisenhower.

Studios, galleries and collectors

The Society of the Four Arts played a key role in boosting the presence of Palm Beach's artist colony, as did the founding of the Norton Gallery of Art and School in West Palm Beach.

Palm Beach resident artist J. Clinton Shepherd became director of the Norton Gallery School of Art from 1941-46. A founder and president of the renowned Silvermine Artist's Guild in Westport, Shepherd was an in-demand national book and magazine illustrator who moved to Palm Beach during the 1930s. One of the town's most popular personalities, while at the Norton, the US Sugar Corporation commissioned Shepherd to design a ninety-eight-foot Everglades mural for the Clewiston Inn, now considered a Florida artistic landmark. Along with spectacular murals for Florida and Georgia plantations, Shepherd's landscapes were considered the finishing touch for the island's loggias. His portraits were must-haves for prominent profiles.

Shepherd's studio on Royal Poinciana Way is often credited with being the island's first semi-commercial art gallery promoting the works of other local artists. Grand Rapids businessman and Palm Beach winter resident Orville "Orvy" Bulman held his first one-man show at Shepherd's gallery. Later, working from his Worth Avenue studio for more than thirty-five years, Shepherd and his fellow bon vivants were frequent fixtures at Wertz's, Nando's, Maurice's and Ta-boo.

In 1942, the Worth Avenue Gallery opened under the co-direction of Mary Dugget Benson and Emily Rayner, although it was owned by the elusive Alice Delamar. For the next twenty-

(Left) Top: J. Clinton Shepherd moved to Palm Beach during the 1930s, becoming the Norton Gallery School of Art's first art director. Along with spectacular murals for Florida and Georgia plantations, Shepherd's landscapes were considered the finishing touch for the island's loggias and his portraits were must-haves for prominent profiles. *(Courtesy of the Shepherd family)*

(Left) Bottom Left: A Palm Beach personality for more than four decades, artist Channing Hare's portraits were in demand from Fifth Avenue to Ocean Boulevard. Shown here in 1964 framed by his work before another of his sold-out shows, Channing Hare studied under the renowned George Bellows and Robert Henri. *(Palm Beach Daily News)*

(Left) Bottom Right: Local artist Keith Ingermann, right, became a collectible artist following his shows at the Worth Avenue Gallery and the support of patron Alice Delamar. *(Palm Beach Daily News)*

three years, Delamar's gallery at 347 Worth Avenue introduced the work of Bernard Buffet, Keith Ingermann, Channing Hare, Patricia Massie, Piero Aversa, Ouida George, and Zoe Shippen, along with watercolors by Franz Bueb, who designed *Town & Country* magazine covers. The Worth Avenue Gallery's annual Left Bank-styled clothesline shows drew large crowds, often popularizing the work of unknown artists.

The Palm Beach Art League staged outdoor weekend shows along South Lake Drive and open-air Washington Square-inspired shows around Memorial Fountain. After a 1948 clothesline show along Via Parigi featured the work of nineteen-year-old West Palm artist Keith Ingermann, the artist's stylized Buffet-like work became in demand from Palm Beach to Monte Carlo, where Ingermann eventually moved. By 1952, "Orvy" Bulman had held his third show at the Worth Avenue Gallery. Bulman's shows were pre-opening sell-outs; three years later, Bulman had his first New York show.

In 1960, Palm Beach Galleries opened on Worth Avenue with George E. Vigouroux Jr. as artistic director. The gallery carried on in much the same tradition of decorous work begun by Delamar's venue, featuring Jack Gray's nautical motifs, Pierre Bertrand's seascapes, and Charles Baskerville's magical Balinese subjects. It was owned by several staunch art patrons, among them, Mary Sanford, Diana Manning, Jane Volk, George Warner, Larry Sheerin, Barbara Headley, and Lillian Phipps. In December 1965, Phipps opened her own gallery, Lillian Phipps Galleries, at Royal Poinciana Plaza.

It was at Palm Beach Galleries where the legendary Jimmy Barker worked for more than a decade before opening his own James Hunt Baker Gallery at 337 Worth Avenue. With additional galleries in New York and Nantucket, Barker's gallery was a showcase for more than fifty artists, including "the mystical flamboyant be-jeweled" Piero Aversa, known as the "King of Mykonos." At the time, Barker was quoted as saying, "Art is a world of fantasy. It is a necessary thing."

As much acclaim as these galleries achieved, it was unquestionably Wally Findlay who solidified Palm Beach's standing in the international art scene. A Worth Avenue institution since 1961, Wally Findlay Galleries has successfully cultivated a lasting appreciation for period and contemporary artists, including Jean Dufy, Le Pho, Bernard Buffet, Andre Andreoli, Gustavo Novoa and Nicola Simbari. On his 75th birthday in 1978, Findlay said he focused on Impressionist and post-Impressionist painters because those works were, "the easiest to live with."

Despite Palm Beach's unwarranted repute for decorous inconsequential art, early Palm Beach galleries made room for more serious contemporary expressions. The highly-regarded Hokin Gallery featured works by Kokoschka and Leger. In 1967, Gallery Gemini, Albert Goldman's influential contemporary art venue, held an exhibit "exploring photography as art."

"Gallery life is alive and well on Palm Beach although we still need the type of energy and synergy those past gallery openings created," said Laurel Baker, executive director of the Palm Beach Chamber of Commerce. "Palm Beach galleries are in a unique position to capture the continuing emergence of the international luxury market."

The resort's years as an artist colony make for one of the town's most beguiling legacies, when being a Palm Beach original opened every door in town.

Top: Worth Avenue gallerists Wally Findlay and Simone Karoff, Findlay's executive vice president, put Palm Beach on the international art map. *(Palm Beach Daily News)*

162

Top: Villa Fiori's tiled murals add color and narrative to the garden walls.

Playa Riente, bas-relief plaster sculpture. Percival Dietsch, artist.

III. Scenes

Great Gardens

In today's Palm Beach, super-sized houses flourish unrestrained by reason or means, overwhelming the resort's scenic beauty and diminishing its once extravagant greenery, now designed as much for party tents as parterres. Considering the present allure of accommodating the world's most–coveted mansions, euphoric shops and colossal yachts, it is surprising anyone ever traveled to Palm Beach simply to behold its landscape. And yet, the barrier island's palms, pines and pawpaws were once the only reason to visit this exclusive tropical paradise.

Set apart from the rest of South Florida, Palm Beach's flora thrives despite the relentless salt spray, aphids, whiteflies, offshore winds, blowing sand, and vigilant water restrictions. For within this high-society bastion, slat houses are kept in constant bloom with South African begonias and Amazon cattleyas. Street-side landscapes are perfectly-composed still-lifes with each leaf polished and every blade of grass manicured. Today's Palm Beachers live within their own perpetual Edens behind ubiquitous ficus hedges camouflaging chain-link fences topped with security cameras. These are private wonderlands, suspended in an eternal spring where nature imitates art.

(Left) Top: Garden of Eden, North Lake Trail. In 1887, Charles and Frances Cragin acquired their initial twenty acres of jungle north of today's Palm Beach Country Club that they eventually transformed into a two hundred and fifty acre botanical paradise. Before building Reve d'Ete, their winter home and the era's foremost showcase, the Cragins began importing and planting exotic hardwoods, fruit trees and ornamental plants to such an extent that the federal government declared their lakeside landscape an experimental botanical garden. *(Library of Congress)*

(Left) Bottom Left: Along the Jungle trail, giant banyan trees became tourist attractions. *(Library of Congress)*

(Left) Bottom Right: Cluett Memorial Garden at The Episcopal Church of Bethesda-by-the-Sea.

More than a century ago, Palm Beach was regarded as the garden spot of Florida, ensconced between shell-covered white sand beaches and a freshwater lake with a labyrinth of lake trails and jungle paths leading through cocoanut groves and custard apple fields. Visitors leaned on corpulent tree trunks and perched on limbs as photographers took their portraits, the lakeside jungle's favored souvenir.

On the island's north end, Reve D'Ete, the Charles Cragins' lakeside estate known as the Garden of Eden, showcased such an array of exotic species that it became the North Lake Trail's

major attraction. The Saguaro cactus was imported from Arizona, pineapples from Mauritius, century plants from West Africa, and orchid trees from China. These more striking plants were combined with closer-to-home Caribbean traveler's palms, flowering oleanders, guava bushes, and rows of avocado trees.

Top: Cluett Memorial Garden at The Episcopal Church of Bethesda-by-the-Sea.

Toward the south at Figulus, Oliver Payne Bingham enlisted the renowned Washington horticulturalist, Dr. David Fairchild, to oversee deliveries of towering hardwoods and cycads brought in on steam launches and sailboats from Hawaii and Havana. The island's mangroves and marshes were transformed with stately royal palms, altissimas and cascades of colorful hibiscus and bougainvillea into a forest of foliage as dreamlike as a Rousseau painting. As director of the US Office of Plant Introduction, Fairchild's efforts are now commemorated at Fairchild Tropical Botanic Garden in Miami while Blossom Estate property owners still retain many of the original plantings.

But no sooner had the wilds of Palm Beach been refined and enhanced than the 20th century's blitz of asphalt and concrete uprooted Palm Beach's natural habitats, subdividing and supplanting them with man-made landscapes. Alligator Joe's reptilian sanctuary bog was replaced with the marble-floored patios and Court of Oranges at the Everglades Club. Drawn more from Edith Wharton's taste for Tuscan villas with obelisques and balustrades than Olmstead's prescription for the preservation of natural scenery with sun dials and bird baths, the island's fields of wild roses, lilies and violets were displaced and framed by clipped hedges. Ornamental flowerbeds decorated enclosed patios and courtyards were paved with flagstone and coquina.

House and garden were amassed to form stylized architectural compositions, fanciful tableaux borrowed from renderings of Spanish castles, English manors and Italian palazzos. Casa Bendita's loggias and Casa Alejandro's terraces allowed their owners to winter in Palm Beach, but feel like they were on the Italian or French Riviera. Nearly a century later, these once grand sculpted gardens no longer exist except as lantern slides. Palm Beach still lacks for a transcendent Shangri-La as illusionary as Vizcaya.

The Garden Club of Palm Beach

Although The Garden Club of Palm Beach's annual flower show may no longer be the social summit it was when first held at the Royal Poinciana Hotel's glass conservatories, the island's ruling green thumbs have remained leading advocates to ensure Palm Beach remains a showcase

(Left) Top: Spanish Garden, Garden Club of Palm Beach demonstration garden, The Society of the Four Arts.

(Left) Bottom: Garden Club of Palm Beach. Glee Smith, club president Marion McKinlock, and Ellen Frazer, whose mother Elizabeth Glendinning was the first honorary president of the Garden Club of Palm Beach. *(Lucius Ordway Frazer Collection)*

Top: This landmarked banyan can be found in the parking lot at the Royal Poinciana Plaza.

for escapist landscapes and supernatural settings. In 1929, the Garden Club retained renowned the civic architectural firm of Bennett, Parsons and Frost to draw up the Plan for Palm Beach that continues to be an inspirational roadmap for the town's development.

Several years later, the Garden Club supervised the architectural designs and plantings for several themed demonstration gardens next to the Society of the Four Arts Library.

For the Chinese Garden, Mrs. Lorenzo Woodhouse designed I Ho Yuan, modeled on an 18th century Beijing palace garden. This artful recreation is replete with a classical temple entrance, statuary, and a pond evoking the Zen yin-yang of creation and contemplation. Along with the

(Left) Top: The Pannill Pavilion faces the plaza and fountain donated by Naoma Donnelley Haggin.

(Right) Top: The garden wall at Ceilito Lindo was said to be 17th-century Venetian. *(Historical Society of Palm Beach County)*

(Right) Bottom: I Ho Yuan, Chinese Garden, Garden Club of Palm Beach demonstration garden, The Society of the Four Arts.

papyrus, water lilies and flowering lotus, symbol of spiritual perfection, Buddha's statue is flanked by a dwarf fern-leaf bamboo and a weeping podocarpus with Buddhist pine and aralias placed around the wall.

A few steps from I Ho Yuan, Mrs. Joseph Gunster planned the Moonlight Garden with a spectacular semi-circular garden bench as a centerpiece sheltered with Japanese privet and scented dwarf Asian night-blooming jasmine with a ground cover of fishtail sword ferns. For the Spanish façade garden and patio, Mrs. John S. Phipps was inspired by her own Alhambra-like gardens at Casa Bendita. Tropical blue wisteria, "Queen's wreath," climbs the stucco wall partially covering a stone tympanum above the door inscribed with "Ave Maria plenum gratia …" a Hail Mary entrance. The coral-stoned patio is completed with a garden bench clad with Spanish-blue tiles and terra-cotta pottery surrounded by a profusion of birds-of-paradise, golden shrimp plants, and Philippine ground orchids.

In addition to the seven prototype displays, the organization later acquired three adjacent vacant lots, transforming them into the Phillip Hulitar Sculpture Gardens. These additional areas serve as an outdoor museum, a botanical garden and an urban park. The Pannill Pavilion is a recent addition, an exuberant architectural folly for events and educational programs.

The 1973 Historic and Specimen Tree Ordinance, protecting the town's exceptional greenery, was enacted with the support of the Garden Club. Since then, the Town of Palm Beach Public Works department and the Garden Club of Palm Beach have guided a tree preservation program that now includes nearly one hundred designated trees, protected by annual inspections. Palm Beachers prize their art collections and the resort's gathering of trees may be one of island's most aesthetically significant resources.

The island's magnificent trees were once a main attraction. Hotel guests and visitors perched on limbs and leaned on tree trunks as photographers took their portraits, the ultimate souvenir from the lakeside jungle. Before the craving for ficus hedges, the island's natural profusion of trees and

(Left) Top: Elizabeth Kay, left, was one of the area's prominent green thumbs, having founded what has become known today as the Pine Jog Environmental Center. *(Palm Beach Daily News)*

(Left) Bottom: The courtyard fountain at Buenos Recuerdos on Middle Road.

At Southways, columns form an artful array along the windbreak of Australian pine trees.

massive shrubbery once sufficed. Those that survived storms were later lost to subdivisions and development. The Royal Poinciana Hotel did not survive the century's need to be modern, but a mighty Mysore Fig tree still stands as a landmark, albeit encased within an asphalt parking lot.

Sacred ground

East from where the Royal Poinciana once stood across the sweep of The Breakers golf course, stands the Cluett Memorial Garden, a pristine meditative garden secluded within the grounds of

The Episcopal Church of Bethesda-by-the-Sea Church. With a distinctive reflection pond, the setting is as serene as it was in 1926 when Nellie Cluett dedicated it to her parent's memory.

Consecrated at the same time as the architectural firm of Hiss and Weeks designed the church, the Cluett Memorial Garden was modeled on formal Italian Renaissance gardens. The matching stairs with obelisque finials separate the lower stone-paved courtyard facing the tea house from the upper landscaped parterre centered with a rectangular pond, which extends the full-length of the terrace north-south from a well-shaped fountain down to the larger tiled-basin on the lower level. Conical-roofed gazebos anchor each corner. The garden was designed by Walter Horstman Thomas, a prominent Philadelphia architect known for his church designs. The garden's colorful seasonal flower beds are framed by stands of bougainvillea and hibiscus. A Della Robbia plaque of the Madonna and Child embellishes the east wall near the tea house.

Recreating nature

In 1994, the Preservation Foundation of Palm Beach transformed a mid-town parking lot into Pan's Garden. Just steps from Worth Avenue's couture collections, Pan's Garden is a half-acre upland and wetland preserve established and maintained by the Preservation Foundation of Palm Beach. It showcases more than three hundred varieties of Florida native plants. Named for the statue of Pan designed by Frederick W. MacMonnies in 1890 that graces the entrance pool, the garden's paths and walks meander through an array of endangered species and seasonal displays. There is also a hundred-year-old live oak along with orchids, wild flowers and bromeliads. Educational and community events are held in a central pavilion overlooking an elaborately-paneled wall composed of Portuguese and Mizner-designed tiles salvaged from Casa Apava.

Today, the Royal Poinciana Hotel's magnificent gardens and cocoanut groves exist only in our memory. Only there can we imagine the time when the sun set and twinkling colored lights illuminated the trees as the crowds lined the piazzas and the orchestra began a waltz as hundreds danced beneath the stars on the remote tropical island called Palm Beach.

(Left) Top: Located on Barton Avenue, the garden at Southways features an exedra as an exterior focal point from the 80-foot center hall within the house.

(Left) Bottom: Pan's Garden, Peruvian Avenue at Hibiscus. The Preservation Foundation of Palm Beach converted a Midtown lot into Pan's Garden, a showcase of Early Florida plantings.

Fish Tales

Since in today's fashionable Palm Beach, "Who are you wearing?" is a routinely-asked conversational opener, it might be hard to fathom that more than century ago "What's biting?" was the only question of interest on Palm Beach.

There was a time when nowhere else in the world could you expect to take a wheelchair ride along a jungle trail, dance the turkey trot among the coconut palms beneath the moon and stars, hook a spouse, net blue runners, and land a sailfish.

Sport fishing was among the town's most captivating allures whether trolling along the expansive shell-lined shore, casting a line from one of the ocean or lake piers, or angling offshore for one of the deep sea's biggest billfish.

The Breakers pier

From its inception in 1896 until its destruction following the catastrophic Hurricane of 1928, The Breakers pier made headlines for its "catch of the day," which might have included a four hundred-pound turtle, an eight-foot sailfish or a thousand-pound shark. But it was also one of the Gilded Age's most innovative if not anomalous structures.

Several months after construction began on The Palm Beach Inn, Henry Flagler announced plans to build a pier with a railroad extension that would serve as a port for his newly-established

(Left): The annual Sailfish Derby held off Palm Beach was one of the world's premier fishing tournaments. Between 1934 and 1938, more than 10,000 sailfish were caught off Palm Beach and more than 60 charter boats were operating off the coastline. *(Lucius Ordway Frazer Collection)*

fleet of steamships, according to historian Sue Pope Burkhart's authoritative account published during the early 1970s in the historical journal *Tequesta*. With Capt. J. D. Ross supervising its construction, The Breakers pier formally opened on January 18, 1896 as the Port of Palm Beach. In addition to the iron tracks, the government installed a signal tower to warn mainlanders in case of any anticipated naval invasion.

Twenty years before the Port of Palm Beach was established at its present location, The Breakers pier served Henry Flagler's Palm Beach-Nassau Steamship Line. And as much as Flagler's extension to Key West became known as the Overseas Railway, the hotel's original pier might have been the state's first overseas railway, albeit on a smaller scale, as it was constructed with a thousand feet of tracks, allowing passengers to go directly from their railway cars onto awaiting vessels. The pier's railway tracks were removed shortly after the last sailings from the pier in 1903. Afterwards, the steel-reinforced pier was still utilized as dockage for private yachts, became an extension of the existing boardwalk for guests and residents to enjoy the seashore's scenic panoramas, and provided fishermen prime access to the bountiful fishing grounds near The Breakers reef.

"The sea is so clear a man may drop a dime in more than forty feet of water at The Breakers pier and see it distinctly in the sand," reported *The New York Times*. The alchemy of the Gulfstream current, the north winds, and temperate climate filled Palm Beach's waters with wahoo, kingfish, marlin, sailfish and sharks.

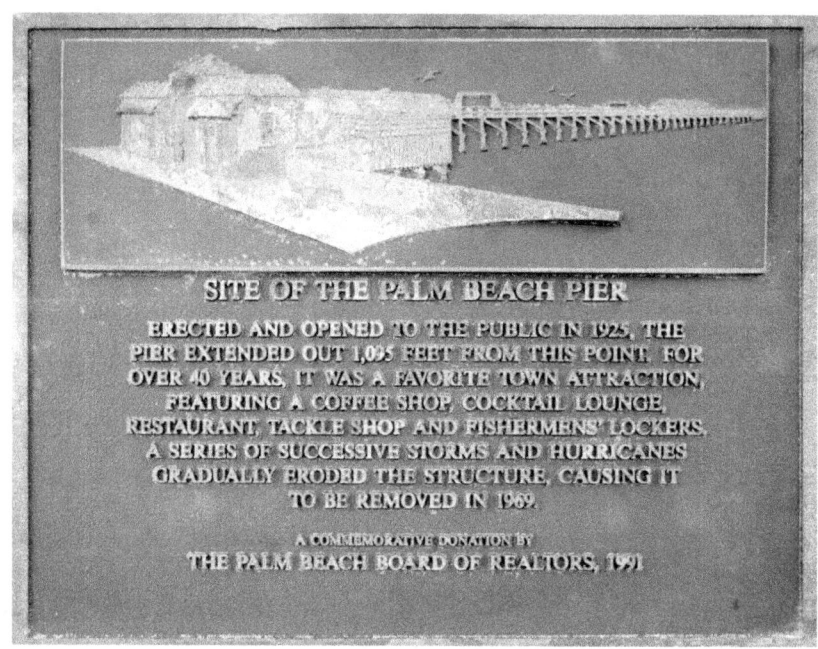

The pier became a popular spot for shark fishing. Once a fisherman hooked a large shark, an attendant in a surf boat harpooned and often shot it. Then, it was hauled up by a windlass installed at the end of the pier. Lucky fishermen were often photographed with their ultimate Palm Beach souvenirs, after the fish were weighed and measured by pier's steward, a representative of the Sailfish Club.

In January 1901, the *Palm Beach Daily News* reported that "Hammerhead Charley" landed his eighth shark of the season off The Breakers pier. The same report made note that the day's haul of amberjacks and Spanish mackerels, along with actor and Henry Flagler-confidante Joe Jefferson's catch of thirty-six bluefish, fifty-seven snappers, and one hundred ten sheepshead, made for what might have been one of the biggest fishing days in Palm Beach's history.

Organized in 1914 at The Breakers, the Sailfish Club maintained the official scales at the pier, the standard for daily and tournament records. Later, when the Sailfish Club moved to Whitehall Hotel before its present North Lake Way location, the Palm Beach Angler's Club took over managing the pier.

The Palm Beach Angler's Club formed in 1924 and was limited to one hundred members. Though sharing the same steward and scales with the Sailfish Club at The Breakers pier, the Angler's Club convened at the Hotel Royal Daneli on North Lake Trail. Both clubs conducted tournaments, often with different equipment standards and awards. In 1932, the clubs merged, becoming the Sailfish Club of Florida. Two years later, the West Palm Beach Fishing Club was organized, convening at the Royal Worth Hotel. By 1935, the West Palm club had four hundred members from West Palm and Palm Beach, and held the Sailfish Derby.

Seasonal storms took their toll on The Breakers pier's structural capacities. Having been rebuilt several times, following the devastating Hurricane of 1928 what remained of the pier was allowed to disintegrate. By then, a new more palatial European style hotel had replaced The Breakers' less imposing wood-frame hotel that was destroyed by fire. And during the mid-1920s, south of The Breakers at the eastern point of Worth Avenue, another fishing pier was built, first widely-known as the Rainbo Pier before becoming the Palm Beach Pier, by Gus "Welcome to our Ocean" Jordahn, who owned the Lido Pool complex across the street.

Left: The Palm Beach pier was one of the town's popular rendezvous spots.

The Palm Beach Pier

Built more than a thousand-feet into the ocean, the Palm Beach pier survived the 20th century's fiercest storms. But when the public pier was closed during the late 1960s, "… nipped by storms and baffled by a changing world," it was the town's increasing sentiment for a more private Palm Beach that turned this popular gathering place and engineering landmark into a postcard from the past.

Although heavily damaged by the Hurricane of 1928, following the storm it was rebuilt into a far more elaborate venue, connected to the Lido complex by a tunnel beneath Ocean Boulevard. Residents and winter visitors reported schools of snappers, sailfish, kingfish, and bonito. A record-breaking forty-five-pound tarpon was caught at the pier. Midnight fishing at the pier became a Palm Beach pastime.

In 1931 "Capt." William D. Gray and Hedley Gillings bought the pier, adding an aquarium with eighteen tanks, including a black-eyed angel fish and a glass-eyed snapper, while increasing the admission charge to twenty-five cents.

Seven years later, Hedley Gillings assumed full control and renamed it Hedley's Pier. On December 16, 1938, Hedley's formally opened, having undergone a major Spanish-style renovation supervised by engineer and contractor Karl Riddle. The modernized facility now contained a cocktail bar, restaurant, package store, a soda bar, and a tackle shop. At the same time, Gillings signed an agreement with the town that should the pier ever be destroyed, it could not be rebuilt and the property would revert to the town.

During World War II, "dim-outs" prevailed along Palm Beach's seashore and the Coast Guard took over the pier's operation. Afterward, the pier regained its popularity among residents and visitors.

The final wave

During the summer of 1946, Hedley Gillings sold the pier for $125,000 to Tom Mathes and Louis and John Agnastopoulus, brothers who owned restaurants in North Carolina. The following year, the partnership sold its interest for $115,000 to Palm Beach Pier Inc., headed by Detroit oil man William Fisher and plumbing magnate Morris Canvasse. This partnership immediately announced plans to further enhance the facility by adding a cocktail lounge and renovating the Oceanside restaurant. The following season, the marine deck cocktail lounge offered full-course dinners for $1.75 and starlight dancing over the ocean until 4 a.m.

But, the pier's vulnerable location would ultimately determine its demise. Hurricanes in 1947 and 1949 destroyed the ends of the pier. Two storms in the 1960s each wiped out another three hundred feet. By 1967, the pier had been sold several times. A winter storm in 1969 left it in shambles. Revitalization plans were scrapped. Later that same season, the Town Council ordered it demolished.

Nevertheless, a company headed by Edwin Sowers and resident Nancy Wakeman presented plans in April 1970 to convert the pier into a private club. Their proposal for reconstruction provided for a new pier, concession stand and public restrooms, as the state health department had ordered the town must provide public restrooms. In July 1974, the Town Council denied the Sowers-Wakeman plans to rebuild the pier. Subsequently, the property was deeded to the town. The pier's pilings stood for another two decades before they were finally blown up; a beach nourishment project in 1995 did away with the last of the pier's visible remnants.

Palm Beach's fishing piers once afforded everyone the same chance of reeling in a marlin or sailfish as they would have from a custom fighting chair aboard a million-dollar Rybovich cruiser. Residents and visitors shared an amiable common ground to share a lifetime of fish tales about the one that got away. With the loss of the fishing piers, Palm Beach's future generations lost a link to a way of life and values now long since gone.

Showplace for Shops

Beaux Arts, Worth Avenue, Phipps Plaza, & Royal Poinciana Plaza

How Palm Beach evolved from a far-flung tropical island known for its jungle trails, ostrich farm, and banyan trees to a fashionable international runway for luxe labels makes for a lesser-told chronicle of the island's commercial retail developments.

Ever since the weekly fashion shows at the Everglades Club became the vogue, and Saks Fifth Avenue packed up its berets and beach pajamas at the Fashion Beaux Arts and put them in the windows at the new Mizner-designed arcade surrounding the club, Worth Avenue has been Palm Beach's showcase for the precious and the pricey.

From Main Street to the Fashion Beaux-Arts

While Worth Avenue prevails as the established most-recognized commercial center of Palm Beach, during earlier years it was Main Street, now Royal Poinciana Way, and the Fashion Beaux Arts-America Building on the North Lake Trail that captivated shoppers among the town's cottage colony and seasonal hotel guests. Before Main Street was widened as a parkway lined with royal palms, its storefronts resembled the cozy shops and comfort-menu restaurants you might find in

(Left): Worth Avenue, January 1964 *(Palm Beach Life)*

PALM BEACH'S SHOPPING CENTER

America's Leaders of Fashion

Every year the foremost Houses of the great cities present their loveliest and newest creations to Palm Beach . . . . . in this beautiful Fashion Beaux Arts.

This Season will see many shoppers here—and many more delightful things to buy! These Shops bring the Modes of the World of Fashion direct to Palm Beach—Modes that foretell the Styles for Spring and give the visitor an opportunity to select her wardrobe from the Shops she knows.

You will recognize these names—here for the Season of 1927

Bar Harbor. But as the Royal Poinciana Hotel and The Breakers expanded and the number of hotels grew, Main Street became a thoroughfare for wheelchairs coming and going to Bradley's Beach Club and to the north of it, the Fashion Beaux Arts Building-America and roof-top theater.

In 1916, Stanley C. Warrick opened the Fashion Beaux-Arts-America Building with what was described as "the finest most exclusive collection of shops in the Western Hemisphere," and the rooftop Beaux Arts Theater, "specially designed for the socially elite." Warrick hired builder George N. Brown and architect August Geiger to create a "building along Mediterranean lines of Spanish architecture," that would be stucco-finished with "bright hues, not flashy." Set in the center of a lush landscaped garden parcel with two hundred forty-five feet of lakefront, the two hundred ten-foot-by-two-hundred-eight-foot "palatial building" made for twenty-five-thousand square feet of retail space accommodating twenty shops. Thus, though Addison Mizner's design for the Everglades Club is most often credited with popularizing the Spanish style, it was actually August Geiger who introduced the town's most prominent stucco-and-barrel tile building several years before Mizner.

Initially, the Fashion Beaux Arts attracted Fifth Avenue's eminent purveyors. Arnold Constable, Theodore Starr, Mme. Helene Rubenstein, and Lanson & Hubbard joined Bonwit & Teller at the town's first "shopping center." In 1925, when the Mizner-Singer development along Worth Avenue began to draw crowds away from the Beaux Arts, the developer enlarged his lakefront presence. Warrick added a California Mission-style improvement called the Seminole Arcade, a string of shops that now extended the complex from the Lake Trail to Bradley Place. By 1930, there were seventeen shops, along with the theater and the chic Colony Club, including Grande Maison de Blanc, J. J. Slater, Best & Company, the Little Pajama Shop, and Tat Saunders. Despite these competitive efforts, Worth Avenue thrived and dominated the seasonal market. The Beaux Arts transitioned into a residential complex before the wrecking ball made way for multi-story apartments.

(Left) Top & Bottom: The Fashion Beaux Arts European-styled shopping complex was located along the Lake Trail between the Mayflower Hotel and the Palm Beach Hotel. Developed by Stanley Warrick and designed by August Geiger, the Beaux Arts, which included a theater and the popular Colony Club, was the premiere shopping and entertainment center until Worth Avenue's popularity brought on its demise. *(Historical Society of Palm Beach County)*

Worth Avenue

Nearly a century ago, Worth Avenue was a dirt path leading to Alligator Joe's menagerie. Today, as the commercial centerpiece for one of the world's fashion capitals, the palm-lined runway is swarming with social lions draped with diamonds and gold, the place to see and be seen and where you could never be too thin or your wallet too thick.

Always more than the stucco-and-barrel tile that most often characterize it, Worth Avenue is a multi-dimensional four-block collaborative spanning a quarter mile from ocean-to-lake. The street's commercial and residential buildings are an assortment of scale and style, Modern and

(Left) Top Left: Tiffany, 259 Worth Avenue.

(Left) Top Right: Via Mizner, view from sheltered walkway to courtyard shops.

(Left) Bottom: Via Mizner, entrance from Peruvian Avenue.

(Right) Bottom: At night, Worth Avenue takes on an otherworldly ambience.

Mediterranean. both public and private. The avenue's facade of recognizable chi-chi luxe logos is as captivating as the must-have accessories uncovered in less familiar off-street courtyard boutiques. This sometimes incongruous mix observes the delicate balance between attracting everyday people — window shoppers who ask "How much?" and satisfying those who have everything, its well-heeled residents who at Chanel or Jimmy Choo's ask, "How much for all of them?"

On an island where houses are screened by impenetrable walls and hedges, and many families seclude themselves for generations within the confines of private clubs, Worth Avenue is the town's most accessible social barometer and most observable architectural venue. Visitors can glimpse the blueblood convent-styled Everglades Club and then step into the labyrinths of vias that twist and turn with silks and sapphires capped with upper-level apartments and offices. Here, the Loggia Lounge and Patio Marguery were once the dimly-lit spots for discreet trysts and nightcaps.

Or, the adventuresome can step up to the bar at Ta-boo, a 1940s retro rendezvous designed by architect Gus Maass. After hearing tales of when The Coconuts held their infamous New Year's Eve soirees in the Tahiti Room, a visitor can explore the "Palm Beach Whites," the street's more Eisenhower-era 1950s buildings with large plate-glass windows. Sheltered by a Havana-brown canvas awning, Maison Maurice's flawless chalk white smooth façade is bordered with decorative pilasters, crowned with a distinct elliptical parapet, its jewel box windows surrounded by unfilled stressed travertine.

Although Tiffany & Co. introduced a jewelry line designed by architect Frank Gehry, best known for his bold geometric juxtapositions, each Tiffany store is modeled on its Fifth Avenue flagship's understated Deco façade designed by Cross & Cross in 1940. It features an elaborated central entrance with stainless or silver doors topped by the signature verdigris Atlas figure shouldering a large Tiffany clock, surrounded paned glass and flanked with showcase windows. For its Worth Avenue presence, Tiffany's maintained its traditional store front by repeating familiar motifs seen from Tokyo to Greenwich, adapted with a Mediterranean coral stone-clad veneer and corner showcase windows shaded with Tiffany-box blue awnings.

Situated at the prominent vortex of South County Road and Worth Avenue, the Worth Avenue Building is a mixed-use three-story 1950's flat-roofed commercial building wrapped with street level plate-glass retail windows set below horizontal offices windows within frames of molded concrete. A bold departure from the avenue's fabled historical styles, the climate-controlled building is a modernist triptych composed of concrete, glass and asymmetrically-patterned brick veneers.

Along the oceanfront, Winthrop House is a 1960s multi-story curvilinear condominium designed by Howard Chilton. It overlooks the Midtown beach where two of the town's most popular attractions, the Palm Beach Pier and Gus's Baths, once stood. The western point overlooking the marina is secured by the Streamline-style Riviera apartments detailed with right-angled eyebrows and cantilevered balconies.

Worth Avenue's architectural crown jewel, the former Greenleaf and Crosby, is a Deco Moderne-styled storefront contained within a Mediterranean Revival building. Florida's oldest jeweler opted for an elegance found on the Place Vendome, a black granite façade trimmed in Monel, a precursor to stainless steel named for Ambrose Monell, a Palm Beacher who at the time was president of the International Nickel Company.

Palm Beach's El Dorado is as well known for its architectural follies as its street battles over window dressings and who's in and who's out. Some publicized run-ins were so devastating, store owners called for priests to administer last rites for the avenue. "Vulgar and disgraceful," decreed haute couture maven, Martha Phillips, the Queen of Worth Avenue, when The Limited Express dressed mannequins in jungle prints during the 1980s. This snafu caused the avenue to dictate new design guidelines prescribing the need for "rhythm," the use of "yellow, green, mauve, blue, pink, light pastels and white as the official Palm Beach colors," and forbidding anything "plastic, fiberglass, or shiny."

Even more heated was the row over the arrival of Neiman-Marcus. Shopkeepers claimed the department store would taint the avenue's treasured mix. Most recently, there was a prolonged Starbuck's squabble. The street's upper crust Old Guard steamed that a Venti Espresso Macchiato would lead to the avenue's imminent collapse.

However resistant, Worth Avenue ensures its longevity and status by accepting changes in taste and standards, no longer "The Mink Mile," once reserved for grand dames. Instead, it embraces Rodeo Drive and Madison Avenue along with its resort brands. The Alibi, Thrift, Inc., and the Prep Shop are memories; Ralph Lauren and Ferragamo have taken their place. Au Bon Gout, Hattie Carnegie and The 400 have vanished, making way for Hermes, Chanel and hedge-fund titans.

Phipps Plaza

With Worth Avenue's popularity growing and the 1920s unconstrained economic heyday apparently having no end, the Palm Beach Company, one of the Phipps family's real estate concerns along with its Bessemer Properties, built Phipps Plaza. Inspired by Addison Mizner's mixed-use vias, Phipps Plaza's detached configuration of commercial and residential buildings was a panoramic progression from the North Lake Trail's Beaux Arts shops and Howard's Major's close-knit Major Alley enclave.

Situated between the rapidly-emerging Worth Avenue and the town's traditional Main Street and "hidden by a prolixity of tropical flowers," the cluster of shops, townhouses and apartments was first known as "Circle Plaza," for the inner-ring road that connected the necklace of buildings to County Road.

By the 1930s the Palm Beach Company had erected twenty "Old World" buildings, a composition that fifty years later would be designated as the town's first historic district. And unlike its predecessors, for the most part the work of one architect, the Palm Beach Company ensured a more eclectic pastiche by engaging not only Mizner and Wyeth but also the work of Treanor & Fatio. This blend of styles created a unique ambience where its office spaces, once described as "the aristocracy of winter enterprises," continue to attract a network of architects, builders and interior designers.

Plaza booms

In 1924, the Palm Beach Company retained architect Addison Mizner to design its first improvement, The Plaza Building, although later, Marion Sims Wyeth would design a cluster of the plaza's defining smaller buildings. Built in the Spanish style replete with arcades and distinctive tower, the Plaza extended north along South County Road to Seaview Avenue. Altered over the years, the building has retained its original character although a central three-portal arcade has been completely removed. It once extended over the sidewalk along County Road with an upper-level office.

(Left) Top & Bottom: Phipps Plaza. Although designed only six years apart, because the two Mizner-designed buildings at the entrance drive leading into Phipps Plaza were built during dissimilar economic times, their aesthetic balance is worlds apart.

The Mizner-designed Plaza Building's first-floor housed Brook's Brothers, Udall & Ballou Jewelers, Nestle's hair salon, and Bonwit Teller's, previously located at the Beaux-Arts Building. The interior of Bonwit's with its metal chairs and carved-glass columns was designed by Whitman & Goodman, New York architects. Above the shop, the offices were primarily used by the building trades, among them, the offices of H. C. Bartholomew, Chalker & Lund, C. G. Warner, DaCamera-Chace, landscape architect Charles Perrochet, and the architectural firm of Volk and Maass.

The following year, according to the Preservation Foundation of Palm Beach's records, Wyeth designed an ensemble of buildings around a central park bordered by a drive named Plaza Circle. This ensemble included No. 206 for Lillas Piper; No. 232 for the Flamingo restaurant, later La Chaumiere; No. 209 at the plaza's northwest corner for the Palm Beach Company's own offices; and, No. 235 for Daniel H. Farr. Next, Wyeth completed drawings for a house at No. 208 for physician Hobart Warren and the Pelican Lodge four-unit apartments at No. 236. In 1927, the Treanor & Fatio architectural added their office building to the picturesque ensemble.

Next door to Brooks Brothers, the Jaeger shop offered houndstooth checks, polka dots, and tartan plaids. Pym's sold pearl necklaces and diamond pins to accessorize silk sport shirts, woolen sweaters and camel's hair jackets. Fahda Jabaly's marketed tomato red linen gowns, "rest gowns," later called negligees, and the "bar dress," labeled "society's pet frock." Nestle's beauty salon specialized in permanent waves. With galleries in Barcelona and New York, the Montllor brothers operated the Spanish Antique Shop at 200 Phipps Plaza.

In 1929, along South County Road on the north side of Seaview Avenue, the Palm Beach Company added three more commercial buildings. Burdine's occupied 228-230 South County Road. The James McCutcheon Company moved from the Beaux-Arts Building to fill the other space along the street.

The following year, E. F. Hutton announced that in addition to agencies at The Breakers and Hotel Royal Poinciana, it commissioned Addison Mizner to design a new two-story quarry-keystone office building at 264 South County Road. Hutton's office building made for a distinctive entrance leading into Phipps Plaza. Built for an estimated $35,000, the building contained a large boardroom and four offices on the ground level with smaller offices above, making for what would

(Right): Phipps Plaza, arcade entrance from South County Road.

200

become one of Mizner's final Palm Beach designs. During the 1940s, this one-of-a-kind building became Finchley's, a popular boutique-restaurant lounge, later evolving into what has become the 264 restaurant.

The Addison Mizner-designed buildings at the entrance to Phipps Plaza, having been saved from the fate of Royal Palm Way's neighboring concrete canyon, are emblematic of Palm Beach's precarious balance of excess and restraint, pitting the 1924 Plaza Building's animated high-style Spanish style against the E. F. Hutton building's restrained functionalism.

Along with the Beaux-Arts Building & Seminole Arcade and Worth Avenue, the Phipps Plaza emporiums flourished during a Palm Beach season when as many as ten trains daily brought thousands of vacationers for holidays at the resort's thirty hotels and a like number of small apartment houses. But with the onset of World War II and changing tastes, the Beaux-Arts and Phipps Plaza's waned in commercial appeal while Worth Avenue was able to sustain its economic draw.

Nevertheless, during the late 1950s, the Phipps family interests decided to veer from Palm Beach's more established European approach to development and introduce a suburban shopping center with a parking lot. However architecturally understated and refined, the center reflected the post-war era's rationale that the automobile dictate commercial architectural design.

Royal Poinciana Plaza

After the Palm Beach Towers opened as the nation's largest hotel-apartment resort in 1955, Bessemer Properties proceeded with developing the adjacent vacant property into a shopping plaza and theater, to be built on the southwest corner of Cocoanut Row and Royal Poinciana Way. Its low profile maintained the views for the multi-story apartment buildings. The plaza's matching commercial buildings were sited in a similar east-west configuration as The Tower's pair of H-shaped buildings. But, in contrast with The Towers, connected by a two-level center concourse that faced Cocoanut Row, the shopping plaza placed its side elevations onto Cocoanut Row, turning its parallel facades north and south. Thus, the bookend buildings became the centerpiece for a vast asphalt parking lot with an encircling roundabout.

(Left): Royal Poinciana Plaza, Cocoanut Row at Royal Poinciana Way.

The Royal Poinciana Plaza's large plate-glass display windows and sea of asphalt ushered in Palm Beach's tail-fin era, when shoppers in their Imperials or Lincoln-Continentals could drive right up to a shop and park. The experience was nothing like Worth Avenue, where parking was at a premium and display windows were retrofitted into jewel-box buildings. While the plaza may have enjoyed some early economic enthusiasm, by the mid-1970s some tenants were eager to return to Worth Avenue. Since the demise of town-serving retail venues, supplanted by national and international logos, the plaza now primarily houses real estate offices, restaurants and personal service outlets. These professionals may not have a need for the structural dynamic of oversized plate-glass windows.

The plaza's north and south buildings feature matching two-story porticos with upper-story horizontal glass window bands and molded pediments set on columns finished with composite capitals. These decorative composite capitals were manufactured during the 1950s and were not modeled from any known actual historical classic order. The bands of upper-story horizontal windows and plate-glass display windows are related more to shopping centers in Palm Beach Gardens than the Regency era's quaint shoppes and boutiques. And however much the Landmarks Preservation Commission's designation report makes numerous references to the plaza's inspired Regency architecture, upon more in-depth scrutiny it may be only the building's silhouette that evokes the 1820s. The complex's substance and details are clearly 1950s.

(Left) Top: 264 South County Road. Now a restaurant, the building first housed the brokerage offices for E. F. Hutton.

(Left) Bottom: The Royal Poinciana Playhouse was once a valuable addition in making the Plaza a commercially-viable venture.

(Right): The Royal Poinciana Plaza has always attracted an eclectic mix of shops.

Reel Life in Old Palm Beach

If idyllic sunny seaside winter days and mild moonlit nights dancing beneath the stars were not enough of a fantastic escape from the harsh reality of Northern cities, Palm Beach was once as entranced with Hollywood moviemaking and silver screen legends as the rest of the country.

Palm Beachers dressed to the nines for afternoon matinees or gala searchlight premieres at one of the island's four movie theaters, and they were thrilled to get a glimpse of silent-era stars shooting scenes on Midtown's beach. They mingled with studio moguls at Ta-boo and were flattered to find their town the subject of the latest wacky romantic comedy, or see themselves portrayed as carefree playboys, scheming widows, and happy-go-lucky heroines. There was a time when film buffs could watch Douglas Fairbanks in *The Gaucho*, Gary Cooper in *Beau Sabreur*, and Jean Arthur in *Husband Hunters* within a few blocks of Main Street.

By 1925, The Stanley Company, owned by Palm Beach resident Stanley C. Warrick, operated all of the theaters in Palm Beach and West Palm Beach. Warrick offered first-run star-studded attractions for the island's seasonal venues at the fashionable Beaux Arts Theatre and the dazzling Diamond Horshoe at the Paramount Theater, "The Milionaire's Movie Theater." The town also originally had a nickelodeon, although the first movie tickets may have actually cost a dime.

(Left) Top: Palm Beach's four movie theaters once attracted several thousand people daily to the area around Royal Poinciana Way *(Palm Beach Daily News)*.

(Left) Bottom: Once Main Street's neoclassical-style showplace, the 800-seat Garden Theatre featured comfortable seating and an orchestra. Today the Palm Beach Book Store is located on the former theater's street level. *(Historical Society of Palm Beach County)*

At the onset of the 1930s, Warrick's company went bankrupt. The national Sparks' chain acquired the Paramount and the Garden as part of its one hundred and twenty-theater monopoly. Eventually, as the Town of Palm Beach grew disenchanted with being the backdrop for screenplays and providing entertainment venues where just-any-someone could buy a ticket, its fascination with filmdom faded and charming movie theaters vanished.

North Lake Trail's Beaux Arts Theatre

In 1916, impresario Stanley C. Warrick opened the Fashion Beaux Arts shopping center on North Lake Trail, designed in the Spanish style by architect August Geiger. Having proclaimed Palm Beach "the winter fashion capital of the world," Warrick built the two hundred-twenty-five-seat Beaux Arts Theatre as a rooftop addition to his popular arcade of New York and Parisian-style shops. In 1917, the Beaux Arts Theatre was leased to showman Carl Kettler Jr. whose father was famed actor Joseph Jefferson's valet.

The "roof movie," as locals called the Beaux Arts, offered three showings daily, usually accompanied by Pathe news films, Krazy Kat cartoons, or comedic shorts. An orchestra played before each movie and a Wurlitzer organist played along with the captioned silent films. Along with the town's hotel ballrooms, the Beaux Arts was also one of the town's earliest venues for charitable fundraisers.

In 1923, the Beaux Arts promised to run "only motion picture plays deluxe with stars," such as Pola Negri, Norma Talmadge and Mae Murray. The venue's popularity peaked when the Colony Club, a chic Café Society nightclub, was added as part of the shopping center's Seminole Arcade. The Colony introduced a new rolling stage that on cue enabled the entire floor of the orchestra shell to be rolled out into the middle of the dance floor. As dreamlike as a photoplay, antique amber lanterns lit the pelican fountains within the surrounding gardens while the club was bathed in green and amber spotlights with rose and purple lights "to emphasize shadows."

Main Street's Garden Theatre

Built by town councilman J. T. Havens at a cost of $75,000, the eight hundred-seat Neoclassical style Garden Theater opened on Main Street in 1922. The premiere presentation was "The Affairs of Anatol," producer Cecil B. DeMille's classic film about adultery starring Gloria Swanson. Between reels, a seven-piece orchestra kept the audience entertained. The lobby was decorated with a gallery of original oil paintings depicting Hollywood stars. Later, Havens leased the facility to Warrick who charged forty-cents for a ticket to the far more extravagant Garden where the seats were two-inches wider and three-inches farther apart than those at the rival Beaux Arts.

After the Sparks theater chain took over bookings, the Garden never regained its former appeal. Havens was granted a nightclub license in 1935, foreshadowing the end of the Garden's history as one of the town's movie meeting places. Four years later, the Chambord restaurant opened, offering haute French cuisine and gypsy violinists. During the mid-1950s and for the following decade, Trosby Auction Galleries conducted its lively estate sales. Quite often, Trosby's auctioneer offered a last chance to buy furnishings from Palm Beach's most imposing settings, as Casa Bendita's now priceless artifacts were sent packing at hammer prices.

The Paramount Theatre

Designed by the renowned set designer and architect Joseph Urban, and built by the Sunrise Corporation as the focal point of a sophisticated mixed-use development for $300,000, the Paramount Theatre formally opened on January 9, 1927 with *Beau Geste* starring Ronald Colman. The distinctive Mediterranean Moderne-styled Paramount Theatre was financed by a local consortium headed by E. F. Hutton and J. Anthony Drexel Biddle Jr. It was also a Stanley Warrick-run operation.

The landmark destination was topped with a distinctive decorative copper-sheathed dome. The complex's triangulated façade separated the theater from the street with a sweeping arch of shops on the ground level and apartments and offices set above them.

Because film making was transitioning from silent-era flash cards to synchronized dialogue, Urban crafted a meticulous interior as functional as it was artful, outfitting it to accommodate a full orchestra for live events, an organ, and audio speaker systems for the coming projected sound-on-film movies.

In a 1929 Theatre Arts magazine article, Joseph Urban described the inspiration for the Paramount's dreamlike silver and green interior palette as "Life [that] is leisured and sunny… the beauties of nature – the palms, distances, the deep-blue sky." For what some believe was the architectural precedent for the architect's Ziegfeld Theater in New York, the picture palace's "Diamond Horseshoe" configuration featured seating for one thousand eighty with one hundred

(Left) Top & Bottom, (Right): The Paramount Theatre's interior was as imaginative and fantastic as the era's best-known picture palaces. *(Library of Congress and Paramount Theatre Collection)*

and fifty-six raised box seats set in a U-shape from both sides of a wide balcony divided by arches into semi-private loges.

For many seasons, opening nights featured searchlights shimmering through the night sky over Palm Beach adding to the resort's unearthly allure. Flo Ziegfeld produced some of Palm Beach's first large-scale charity events on the Paramount stage where the era's best-known entertainers performed. In 1929, a part-silent and part-talkie screen version of *Showboat*, starring Joseph Schildkraut, had its national premiere at the Paramount.

Interest in the Paramount diminished as living room television sets became the preferred entertainment option. Placed in the National Register of Historic Places in 1973, at one point years later the Paramount complex was considered by the Town of Palm Beach as a possible new Town Hall. With its Urbanesque interior details gutted and removed, the former theater has been home to the Paramount Church, civic organizations, specialty shops and art galleries since 1994.

The Colony Theatre

Surprisingly, another movie theater opened on Palm Beach after World War II. Located at 244 Sunrise Avenue, a block west of the Paramount, the Colony Theatre opened in January 1948. The Colony's patrons were afforded air-conditioning, something earlier more luxurious venues lacked. Built and owned by Elias Chalhoub, the venue was leased to R. R. Thomas with the Sparks Theater circuit.

During the 1950s, when evening tickets were seventy-five cents for adults and twenty-five cents for children, thriller and action films were shown in Cinemascope and Technicolor. Howard Hawks' *Land of the Pharaohs* was advertised as actually filmed in Egypt with "a cast of thousands." During the next decade, the Colony Theatre was part of the General Cinema Corporation's circuit of seventy-two theaters and fifteen bowling alleys, including the Carefree in West Palm Beach. Before it was demolished in 1971, the Colony was known for showing, at times, noted art-house and foreign films.

Lights! Camera! Action!

Not only was movie-going a popular diversion from the social obligations of the Palm Beach season, the movie colony's glamorous flashbulb presence enhanced the resort's starry nights. Greta

Garbo could be glimpsed coming-and-going at the Whitehall Hotel. Joan Crawford tanned in the lounge chairs at Nate Spingold's pool on Wells Road. Samuel Goldwyn often edited screenplays sheltered within his beachside cabana at the Bath & Tennis Club. Charles Munn's invitation to dinner-and-a-movie at Amado was one of Palm Beach's coveted invitations for visiting royals and screen legends.

Palm Beach was also a popular setting and focus for big screen plots. In March 1926, film star Bebe Daniels accompanied by forty members of her production crew checked in to the Palm Beach Hotel. The entourage spent several weeks filming *The Palm Beach Girl*. After shooting at the Stotebury's El Mirasol estate, Daniels and her crew set up action shots on Lake Worth, much to the wide-eyed wonder of residents.

Above Left: *The Palm Beach Girl* was filmed in Miami Beach and Palm Beach, where El Mirasol became part of the scenery.

Above Right: *The Palm Beach Story* was a popular 1940s film described as a "screwball comedy." *(Library of Congress)*

As *The Palm Beach Girl* headed for theaters across the country — critics called it "breezy and giddy" — W. C. Fields and Louise Brooks arrived in town to film "bathing shots" for *It's the Old Army Game*. During the early 1940s, Palm Beach was once again on every marquee. Preston Sturges' comedy *The Palm Beach Story*, starring Claudette Colbert and Joel McCrea, put the island in the dazzling limelight in theaters from Peoria to Albuquerque.

Later, Social Register greats were among first-nighters when Cordelia Drexel Biddle's book, *My Philadelphia Brother* opened as a play followed by the movie, *The Happiest Millionaire*. Audiences could not stop laughing at her family's madcap escapades, led by her brother, Anthony J Drexel Biddle, Jr., one of Palm Beach's social icons. Biddle was a founder of the Bath & Tennis Club and the Oasis Club. Opening to favorable reviews and large audiences, the film about the Biddle family's peccadilloes was appropriately nominated for an Academy Award in the Best Costume Design category.

But Palm Beach's enthrallment with glamorous movies didn't carry forward to more recent decades. The town's new prevailing attitude resembles more of a gated residential homeowner's association than an international resort destination. In 1988, the town approved new controls on commercial film production. Many residents labeled moviemaking on Palm Beach streets "a potential threat to public safety." In claiming the town's "dignity" was at stake, some residents asked for a total ban on commercial filming on the island.

Since then, the town has held to the belief, as some residents voiced more than thirty years ago, "Palm Beach is not a movie set."

(Left): Although the Beaux Art and the Garden lacked for searchlight premieres that made the Paramount a Rolls-Royce destination, they were still popular venues.

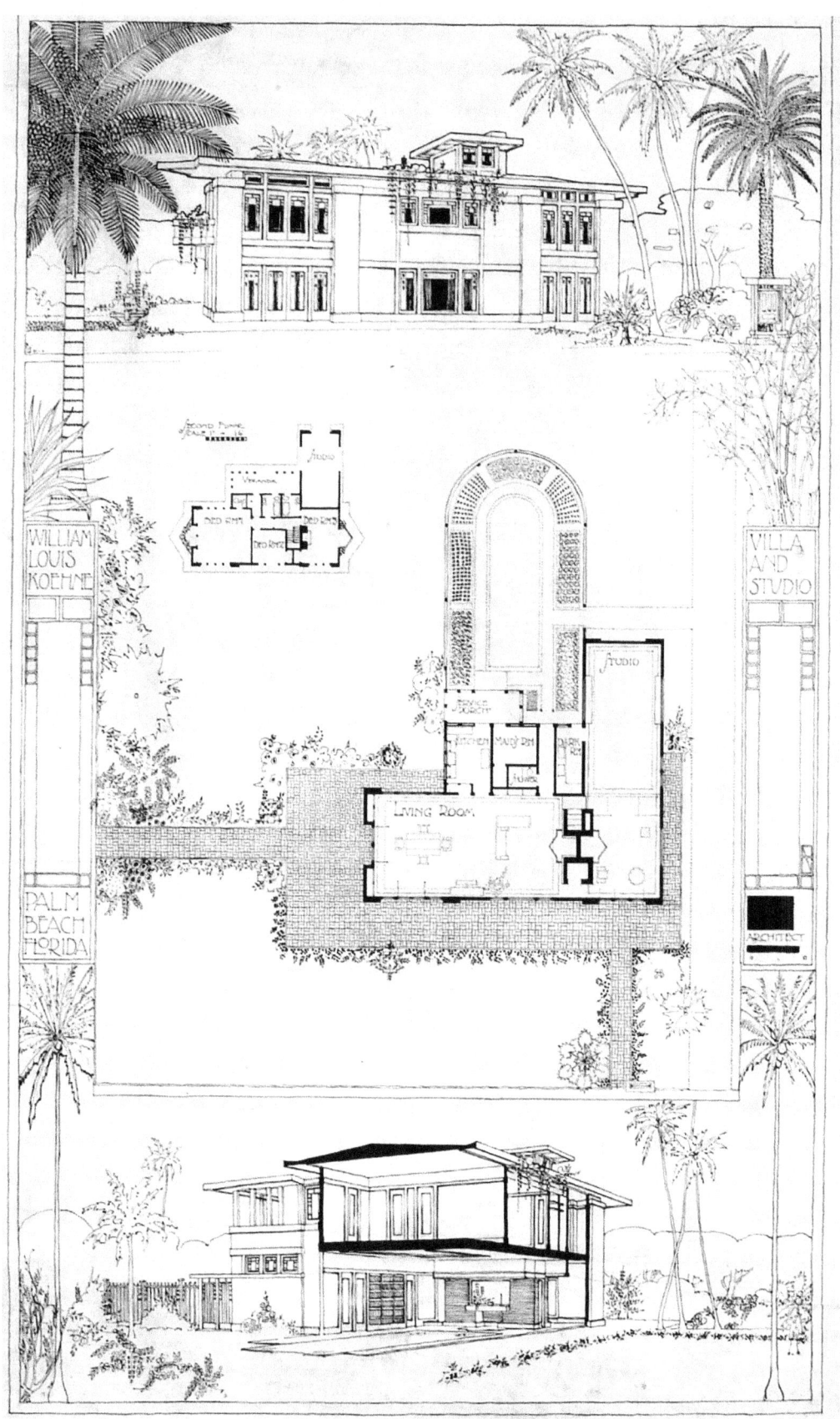

Palm Beach Modern

Palm Beach's architectural tradition is best known for its Mediterranean Revival adaptations. Describing itself as "a Mediterranean-style mecca of architectural beauty," the town has a passion for the artifice of simulated historical facades. During the past twenty-five years, more than five hundred houses have been demolished, many of them Mid-century Modern houses, to accommodate the town's proclivity for contextual new buildings and spec builders' passion for colossal French chateaus, Venetian villas, and over-sized Bermuda bungalows. Thus, Palm Beach's Modernist tradition is a fragmented part of its history rather than present in its streetscapes. An endangered species, their style and size, their raison d'etre, are today grounds for their downfall.

And yet, from the 1930s to the 1970s Modernism prevailed as Palm Beach's paradigm of style. Then, progressive designers, as notable and diverse as Maurice Fatio, Edward Durrell Stone, Alfred Browning Parker, and Richard Meier, fashioned Moderne and Modern houses and buildings rivaling the aesthetic significance of the island's more familiar Old World courtyards and loggias.

Platinum Palm Beachers may be younger than their predecessors but their houses are looking older, too often opting to fit in to this conservative refuge with Renaissance-styled facades and Louis-Louis interiors. Just as the island's streets are no longer filled with Citroens and Isotta Fraschini Cabriolets, its shop windows bare of Palm Beach knickers and Hattie Carnegie's frocks, most of the town's mid-century history has been purged, existing today only in historical photographs, with only a few Modernist buildings designated as landmarks. While never as profuse, visible or

(Left): Villa Zila, architectural plans. Although the architect's name has been blocked out, the Block Museum of Art at Northwestern University credits this presentation drawing of Villa Zila to Walter Burley Griffin and associate Roy Lippincott, dated c. 1913. The drawing was a gift of Marion Mahoney Griffin in 1981. (*Courtesy Block Museum of Art, Northwestern University.*)

accessible as Miami Beach's Deco District or Miami's MiMo District, Palm Beach's collection of Modernist designs is one of South Florida's most refined paradigms of fashion and function.

Years before the first Moderne-style building, yesterday's Palm Beach displayed its inherent enlightened and tolerant nature when two decades earlier it welcomed Villa Zila, a Prairie Modern Wrightian-styled house built along the Midtown oceanfront.

Palm Beach Modern 1914

Villa Zila's provenance is one of Palm Beach's fascinating architectural mysteries with more evidential twists and turns than an Addison Mizner staircase. The spectacular Prairie Modern multi-level house was built in 1913-1914 for William L. and Zila Koehne, a renowned portrait photographer and his socially-prominent wife.

In January 1914, the Koehnes moved into "The Fishbowl," as locals called Villa Zila because of its large glass windows and doors. It was believed to be the first oceanfront house built in Midtown, just two blocks north of today's Worth Avenue. In his *Palm Beach Daily News* ads in 1914, Koehne stated, "The wonderful lighting effects obtainable in Palm Beach cannot be equaled anywhere in the world."

The Koehnes always claimed their unique Palm Beach house was designed by fellow Chicagoan Frank Lloyd Wright who was said to have an office next to Koehne's.

Yet, the available presentation drawings, now held at Northwestern University's Block Museum, have the architect's name blacked-out. And, further clouding the house's origin, the Wright Foundation's current records do not acknowledge the Koehne's Palm Beach commission.

In 1974 the controversy over who might have designed the house became a national story when a demolition permit was approved to level the existing structure, making way for a high-rise condominium. By then, the incomparable Villa Zila had been transformed into the Shorwinds Motor Hotel, a conversion completed thirty years earlier by architect Belford Shoumate for New York hotelier Phillip Reid, who had bought the original house in the 1940s from Mr. Koehne.

At the time of the demolition hullabaloo, scholars noted stylistic details linking the Koehne's L-shaped ten-room South Ocean Boulevard house with Wright's designs for similar houses in the Oak Park suburb of Chicago. They pointed out Villa Zila's original dark brown wood trim and white plaster. They claimed the house's geometric casement windows were "exact matches." Additionally, they focused on the arrangement of the living and dining areas, the two-story open studio, the intersection of the horizontal and vertical planes, and the projecting triangulated side eaves. Villa Zila did display a remarkable similarity with one of Wright's last Oak Park houses, the starkly geometric Balch House designed in 1911.

However much some believed Villa Zila might be Wright's work, there were incompatible elements, such as the observation tower, as well as inconsistent circumstances that might have made it highly improbable for Wright to have actually orchestrated the Palm Beach house's design.

Above: Villa Zila, photograph. *(Historical Society of Palm Beach County)*

Wright intentions

Perhaps, as most came to believe, it was possible that between 1911 and 1912 the Koehnes discussed a possible commission with Wright, as they were well-acquainted; but never settled on any firm agreement or plan. A sketch of the Palm Beach house by Wright has never been found or authenticated.

Also, there may have been a misunderstanding in which the Koehnes thought the house was a Wright-design when actually because of the architect's growing fame he was on the go much of the time, leaving the actual design work to his staff. When Villa Zila might have been designed, Wright had left his Oak Park studio under the supervision of Hermann V. von Holst and his draftsmen, particularly Walter Burley Griffin and his wife Marion Mahony Griffin, who was one of Wright's principal delineators.

Marion Mahony Griffin, an MIT graduate, was one of the nation's earliest prominent women architects. She and fellow Wright draftsman Walter Burley Griffin married in 1911. At the time, it was not unusual for the Griffins to render drawings once Wright had done a sketch, especially in the hectic period after 1909. When Marion Griffin donated the Villa Zila drawings to the Block Museum, although the architect's name was hidden, she stated it was husband's work.

Then, to add another level of uncertainty, according to the Koehne's son, Jack William Louis Koehne, his parents had first offered the commission to Louis Sullivan.

Nevertheless, if Villa Zila had been designed by any one of the famous Chicago Three — Sullivan, Wright or Griffin — Villa Zila would be assured a significant page in the nation's Modernist architectural history.

(Left): 1221 North Lake Way. Fore N' Aft Front entrance. Interior staircase. Façade.

From MedRev Mansions to Moderne

Much of Palm Beach's early 20th-century resort architecture was indistinguishable from Newport and Bar Harbor, awash with New England clapboard cottages, vernacular bungalows, and Beaux-Arts Revivals designed by New York and Philadelphia architects. Then, in 1918, Addison Mizner, a California architect, made popular a stucco-and-barrel tile skyline, influenced as much by Florida's Spanish heritage as convents in Seville.

When the 1930's "Less is more" concept shifted housing styles toward more modest, less formal houses, Palm Beach's walled castles became white elephants. No longer the exclusive enclave of the more staid East Coast social establishment, the resort became an international playground, broadening its stylistic motifs with British Colonial, Georgian, Monterey, Regency and Bermuda designs.

During the same period that the repetition of these borrowed styles turned streets into wallpaper patterns, the town's Old Guard accommodated new wave designs, amassing an artful collection of Modernist buildings. These sleek white concrete buildings were etched with geometric designs, sculpted with rounded corners and open floor plans, making for sophisticated additions to the town's decorum. The era's Modernist zeitgeist, introduced most visibly by architect Joseph Urban's prescient Moderne flourishes to his escapist Bath & Tennis Club design and picturesque Paramount Theater, made it a popular genre for Midtown's commercial buildings, small hotels, apartments and stylish new houses.

(Right) Top Left: Peruvian Avenue, entrance. Located in the ocean block, this exhilarating Streamline Moderne house has retained many of its original features.

(Right) Top Center: In Midtown, low-rise condos were built during the 1960s, as seen in this color sales brochure rendering of the Brasilia condominium located at 227 Brazilian Avenue.

(Right) Top Right: Designed by architect John Stetson, the Riviera cooperative apartments are a refreshing contemporary design on Worth Avenue.

(Right) Middle Left: South County Road, commercial building, detail.

(Right) Middle Right: Plaza Inn, Brazilian Avenue.

(Right) Bottom: Out of Bounds, Island Road. Although the Landmarks commission did not recently designate the Theodore Buhl house as a local landmark, it is one of Treanor and Fatio's finest Streamline Moderne designs. *(Library of Congress)*

When the 1930s "Less is more" concept shifted housing styles toward more modest, less formal houses, Palm Beach's walled castles became white elephants.

Shortly after the S.S. Normandie set sail and the groundbreaking International-style Mandel House was welcomed as a "a radical departure from the conventional house …," Palm Beach architect Belford Shoumate was designing a house in the town's North End jungle as if it were the Normandie itself. Fore and Aft, as the lakeside house became known, was outfitted with circular windows, metal pipe columns, balconies trimmed like decks and bedrooms resembling staterooms. Originally painted cobalt blue, the house was acknowledged in a House of Tomorrow competition, a model of it appearing at the 1939 New York World's Fair.

Having worked with Joseph Urban in New York and Carlos Schoeppel in Miami, Belford Shoumate designed several of Palm Beach's distinctive Moderne buildings, including a house on Peruvian Avenue, one of Palm Beach's sublime architectural compositions. This Midtown cottage features a curvilinear parapet punctured with portholes and an enriched entrance bordered by multi-colored mosaic tiles expressing the era's artistic flair. Reflecting the Swing Era's cosmopolitan élan and elegance Shoumate's whimsical geometric facade is an artful reminder of when Palm Beach was an international epicenter for design.

At the same time, architect Maurice Fatio was designing The Reef, an International-style mansion on North County Road. Fatio's avant-garde oceanfront for the Vadim Makaroffs — Mrs. Makaroff was Huntington Hartford's sister — was first conceived as a more formal Art Deco design. These plans were shelved when the owners encouraged a more international, sweeping, futuristic approach. The resulting U-shaped house featured a central entrance courtyard, glass block walls, and a twenty-nine-foot picture window for the living room's panoramic oceanfront views. The Reef received the Gold Medal at the 1938 Internationale des Arts et des Techniques in Paris, the same year Rockefeller Center was awarded the grand prize.

For the Theodore Buhls' more starkly Modern house, Out of Bounds, set on Midtown's Island Drive, Maurice Fatio opted for a sleek brick design of angles and curves clad with a brick veneer. The loggia arcs into a sweeping turn along the waterfront in a setting originally designed by the renowned Janet Darling Webel, one of the only mid-century women landscape architects practicing in the United States. Except for an added swimming pool, pavilion, bedroom and loggia extension

(Left) Top: The Southlake, advertising brochure.

(Left) Bottom: 389 South Lake Drive, porte cochere entrance. Howard Chilton, architect.

designed by architect Byron Simonson in 1955, the Buhl house has retained much of its original blueprint. Although Out of Bounds does not enjoy local landmark designation status, its design was one of the World War II-era's most sophisticated, reflecting a time when Palm Beach was at the forefront of the world's social and architectural vanguard.

Another Fatio-designed Moderne masterpiece, Villa Today, was situated in the predominately Mediterranean-styled South End mansion district. "Breathtaking," recalls James Ponce, Palm Beach's town historian, describing the relief panels salvaged from the S.S. Normandie once installed in Villa Today's entrance hall. "It was like stepping into the Jazz Age," Ponce added.

On Worth Avenue, Greenleaf & Crosby's incomparable historic storefront, now Betteridge Jewelers, is a Worth Avenue treasure. Its Art Deco Moderne granite façade was trimmed with silvery-white Monel, patented in 1906 and named for Ambrose Monell (1873-1921), president of the International Nickel Company when the process was discovered. Monel was the first nickel alloy, stronger than steel and more resistant to corrosion than bronze. During the 1950s, stainless steel produced with less nickel reduced the demand for Monel.

From Mid-rise to Modern

Palm Beach's post-World War II economy accelerated due to various factors — faster trains, air travel, and modern conveniences such as air-conditioning. Most importantly, a late 1940's zoning change increasing density in Midtown sparked a building boom for more than two decades. Midtown cottages and villas were demolished. Their individual charm and character were first replaced with low-rise apartments and cooperatives. Soon after, these buildings were leveled, giving rise to higher, even more densely-built condominiums.

Although residents vowed that their skyline would never become another Miami Beach, south of Sloan's Curve was surfaced with a phalanx of high rises and Midtown was pocketed with concrete canyons. On Royal Palm Way, a Mizner-designed oceanfront house was supplanted by a seven-story condominium complex. The condominium became Palm Beach's most popular housing motif.

(Left) Top & Bottom: Hoffman house, Ibis Island. Façade and close-up of detail. Designed by the owner in 1960, Tim and Phyllis Hoffman's house represents one of the town's best remaining examples of Mid-century Modernism.

Soon, Palm Beachers were ankle-deep in shag carpets and wearing palazzo pants to condominium board meetings.

The South Lake Drive marina and lakeside park became a favored setting for sleek Modernist buildings. The Eisenhower-era's Riviera apartments, Nassau Square and the nautical-themed 455 Australian complex provided the background for the next decade's serpentine-curved South Lake condominiums designed by Howard Chilton. The architect's signature undulating walls came to represent the epitome of Palm Beach Modernism.

Howard Chilton, a Palm Beach High School graduate, received a degree in architecture from New York University before establishing his practice on Palm Beach. Sited on long narrow lots, the high-ceiling the Chilton-designed buildings were designed to cash in on the available southeast breezes and panoramic views. This refined aesthetic was woven into several Midtown condominium buildings, including the Southlake and Park Place apartments along South Lake Drive, as visually articulate as any of the town's historical stucco facades borrowed from Spanish squares or Italian hill towns.

Although 389 South Lake Drive has lost its familiar deep blue color and its original horizontal concrete panels have been replaced with a sympathetic aluminum railing, the fifty-year-old co-operative apartment building designed by Chilton remains one of the town's most vivacious models of Mid-Century Modernism. As imaginative today as when it was built during an era celebrated by tail fins, bouffant coiffures, white dinner jackets, and cigarette pants, 389 South Lake has become one of Palm Beach's defining silhouettes. Its sweeping serpentine curve is enhanced by vertically-patterned concrete grilles with jazzy linear designs and a port cochere with unfolding gabled roof lines and trellis-like columnar piers, evocative of the Asian influence on Modernism.

Palm Beach Towers

The Palm Beach Towers is the town's largest and most dominating Modernist design, built where the Colonial-styled Royal Poinciana Hotel stood before it was demolished in 1934. Ever since The Towers was built as an architectural quantum leap from its predecessor, its functional design has attracted the celebrated and the accomplished, including stage-and-screen stars from the nearby Royal Poinciana Playhouse, socially boldfaced names and political power brokers. The world media converged in its Regency Room for Pierre Salinger's press conferences whenever President Kennedy was in town. When the nation's poet laureate, Howard Nemerov, and his sister, legendary underworld photographer Diane Arbus, came to Palm Beach they stayed with their parents, David and Gertrude Nemerov, who lived in a penthouse at The Towers.

Designed by architect John Hans Graham in 1956, and built by Turner Construction, The Towers was the largest apartment-hotel resort in the United States. It was initially planned as a hotel with one thousand five hundred rooms topped by an eighteen-room penthouse with an aviary for the Maharanee of Baroda. But because of market demands, The Towers opened in 1956 with three hundred and sixty rooms managed by the Helmsley organization. Crafted in sharp contrast to The Breakers, its 1920s antecedent, which featured an enclosed Renaissance courtyard patterned after the Villa Medici in Rome, The Towers multi-storied wings were angled and flared along the lake, connected by a central two-story concourse with a floor-to-ceiling glass lobby that overlooked the pool, Intracoastal Waterway and West Palm Beach skyline. Although the allure of Mid-century Modern's style has faded, the Palm Beach Towers remains as smart and stylish and as it was fifty years ago.

While The Towers was considered bold and innovative, its developer, Joseph Mass, retained the legendary Alfred Browning Parker to design his own house with an even more Modernist design on Everglades Island. Described by Parker as his 30-60-90 House, the triangulated framework featured multi-level interiors terraced for function and views. Featured by *House Beautiful* magazine, the Island Road southwest point lot design was selected as the 1957 Pacesetter House of the Year.

"When the steel framing went up, town officials called my parents, asking if they were building a drive-in theater," recalled Leonard Mass. "My parents, traditional New Englanders, were shocked when they first saw Parker's plans. He told them if they didn't like it, he'd buy it. My parents loved the house. It was fantastic," said Mass.

Other innovative residential designs echoed Modernism's functional aesthetic. Architect Gustav Maas's L-shaped corner house on South Ocean Boulevard featured a novel second-story living room. The Bryan House, a Wright-inspired lakeside designed by architect Byron Simonson was clad with Tennessee quarry stone. "Modern and Colorful," read the headline in *Palm Beach Life* magazine. Furnished with rattan, the house featured pink satin chairs, plum-colored walls, chartreuse curtains, and green carpet.

(Above) Top Left: Postcard. Palm Beach Towers, Cocoanut Row.

(Above) Top Right: Developer of the Palm Beach Towers Joseph Mass. *(Courtesy of Palm Beach Towers)*

(Above) Bottom: Palm Beach Towers interior, staircase between lobby concourse and lower-level shops.

(Right): Palm Beach Towers, north corner elevation with balconies.

The 400

Originally designed as apartments for Everglades Club members, the 400 South Ocean Boulevard building is known as Palm Beach's first condominium and widely-believed to be the state's first to incorporate following the passage of Florida's Condominium Act of 1963.

Conceived by its builder in 1958 as "the most splendid and modern building that men, machines and money can erect for Palm Beach's international colony," the six-story International-style

building was designed by Edward Durrell Stone, one of architectural history's most influential 20th-century designers, and landscaped by his son, Edward Durrell Stone Jr. Thirty-five years later, the architect's youngest son, Hicks Stone, a New York architect, restored, renovated and updated the building.

"I respected the original design, realizing the need to install more durable modern materials to ensure more functional 21st-century living, and by revisiting his original drawings, introduced some planned but unfinished details," said Hicks Stone.

Featuring a rooftop pool, slender columnettes, grille work and walkways, the white pavilion's central courtyard water garden is one of the architect's signature elements. The ocean-block symmetrical building was a stylistic progression from Stone's landmark design for the American Embassy in New Delhi, called one of the finest buildings in the world by Frank Lloyd Wright. Later, the motif was reflected in his work at the Kennedy Center for the Performing Arts.

The building became one of many condominiums crowding Midtown and the South End's three-and-one-half-mile oceanfront. Although none of them are as iconic as Stone's work, condominiums became the town's most popular building style, forever transforming the cottage colony's low-profile barrel tile skyline into a refined high-rise international resort while never attaining the airless monolithic scale and claustrophobia of Galt Ocean Mile, Sunny Isles or Singer Island.

The recent demolition of two distinct Mid-century Modern buildings, the Manus House by Alfred Browning Parker and the Streamline Moderne-styled Plaza Inn, both undesignated as local historic landmarks, are a reminder of the town's lack of appreciation for Modernism's important role in the town's architectural history. As builders fill streets with faux Italian and ersatz Caribbean styles, only a few contemporary designs have been built during the past twenty-five years, highlighted by Richard Meier's lakefront geometric collage, Camelot, designed to showcase the owner's art collection.

(Left) Top Left: The 400 Building, 400 South Ocean Boulevard. Exterior, east and south elevations.

(Left) Top Right: Entrance, glass doors looking through to the courtyard from the inside looking out across the courtyard water feature toward the west elevation's port cochere entrance.

(Left) Bottom Left: Situated in the central atrium, a sculptural work is set atop a marble base in the courtyard water feature.

(Left) Bottom Right: The 400's west elevation port cochere entrance to interior courtyard and apartment levels.

Everglades Island

In a place like Palm Beach, which revels in what sets it apart from the rest of the world, where the exceptional, the remarkable, and the uncompromised are commonplace, Everglades Island must be regarded as one of the town's most unique milieus. The subdivision's formation and development, as well as the ongoing redevelopment, make for a fascinating chronicle clearly disparate from the main island's enclaves.

When Bessemer Properties platted and planned Everglades Island during the mid-1930s, its appeal and aesthetic were intended as an understated alternative to the mansionization of Palm Beach, popularized during the previous era. And, for more than half a century, it was this prevailing economy of design and density in a relaxed informal setting in tune with the surrounding elements and environment that attracted residents to the island. But now, for some residents, the size, scale and ornate style of the current redevelopment undermine the concept and rationale that initially led to the island's creation.

From birds and boats to waterfront living

Everglades Island began as one of the tiny natural islands scattered throughout Lake Worth. Several are now flourishing bird sanctuaries, a quagmire of scrub palms and tangle of mangroves that sheltered the wood-frame structures that once housed a boat keeper's cottage and various launches belonging to the nearby hotels.

Left: Aerial. The development of Everglades Island was interrupted by World War II. *(Historical Society of Palm Beach County)*

First known as Lone Cabbage Island, the property was acquired by the Phipps family's Bessemer Properties as part of its Island Road Development. The ground plan was made up of landfills that extended westward from County Road fashioned with bulkheads aligning Island Road along the south edge of the Everglades Club's golf course. The dedicated public road curved south as Tarpon Way, first known as Clement Way, and onto privately-owned Tarpon Island. Continuing farther west over a small bridge onto Everglades Island, the road split into Island Drive that traversed the island from south to north.

Twenty-four-hour dredging and filling transformed the island sanctuary into a manmade, thirty-five-hundred-foot-long residential island. Nearby residents were alarmed by the constant noise from the boats and machinery. But Bessemer's managing director and Town councilman, James F. Riley, who supervised the Island Road development, was able to address the residents' concerns and work continued on what was considered the town's largest residential project since the 1920s.

The work was completed in two stages, with Island Road, Tarpon Way, and the south one thousand feet of Everglades Island was completed first. Only a few houses were built at the onset of World War II before all of the area's construction halted. The south end was not completed until 1946; two years later, the north end was cleared, filled, and secured with a sea wall. Once utilities were installed, Island Drive was paved with turnabouts at either end, landscaped with melaleuca and coconut palm trees.

During the mid-1950s, Everglades Island lots were dotted with low-key island-style houses, patterned after Bermuda, Lyford Cay and Caribbean styles. These less conspicuous seasonal retreats featured more informal interiors, Florida rooms, air-conditioning and modern appliances.

Bessemer sold lots for $17,500 each. Lagoon front lots sold for $165 per front foot; Intracoastal Waterway lots were $190 per front foot. The developer offered lots with the following conditions: No discount for cash, one-third cash balance payable in one to five years at six percent interest, payable semi-annually. All clients were subject to owner's approval. Property was not available for speculative building. Houses were to cost no less than $20,000 and contain no less than thirty-thousand cubic feet. A thirty-foot front setback was required; twenty-foot setback from the lake

(Left) Top: Entrance feature, Everglades Island.

(Left) Bottomt: Aerial. The development of Everglades Island was completed in stages before and after World War II. *(Historical Society of Palm Beach County)*

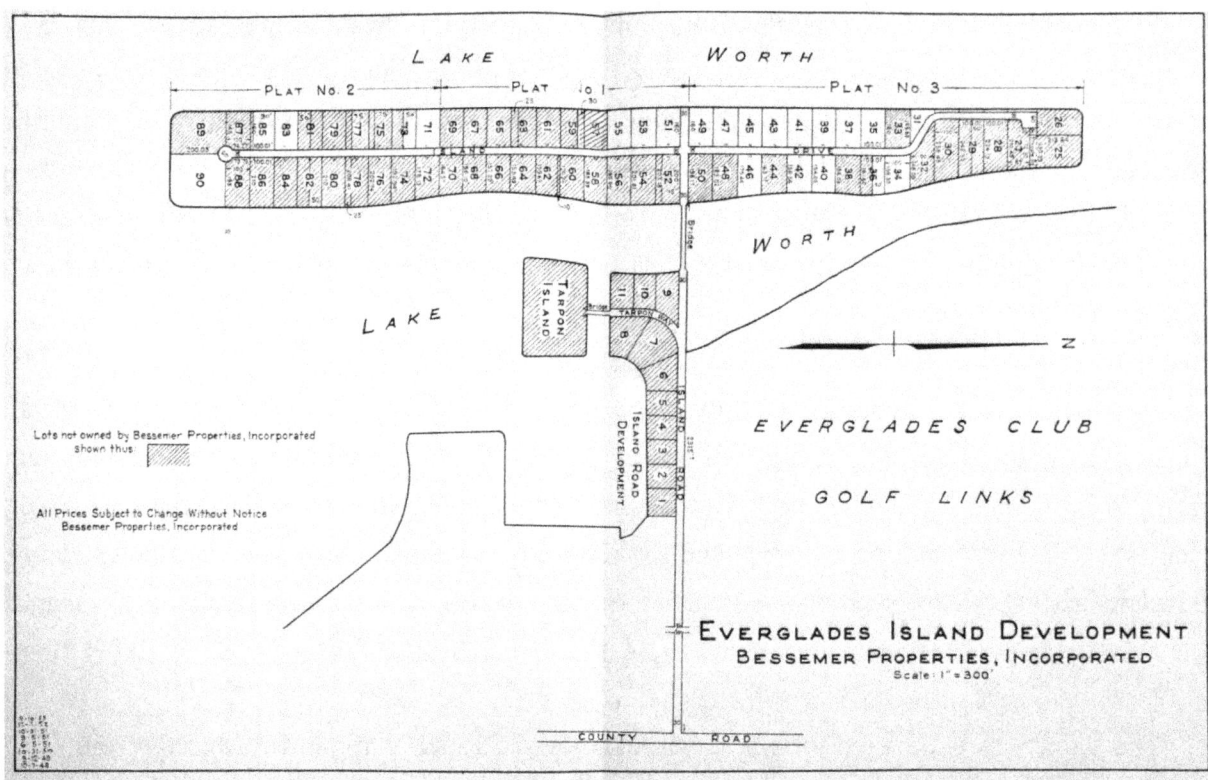

wall; ten-foot side setback; and no garages were allowed that had an opening facing the street.

As the stucco fifty-room white elephants of the 1920s became passé, Palm Beach embraced Modernism. Everglades Island's downsized secluded environment played a part in the resort's movement toward living in a more resourceful resort with villas, small apartments and co-ops.

When Joseph Mass planned to build a house on Everglades Island that would rival the contemporary modernism of his Palm Beach Towers, he and his wife, Henrietta, "Hank," retained Alfred Browning Parker, the legendary architect known for his Frank Lloyd Wright-inspired organic designs.

The result was one of Palm Beach's state-of-the-art houses; its Tropical Modernism featured slanted roof planes, limestone walls, cedar ceilings and enhanced with built-in custom furnishings designed by the architect. Dubbed the "30-60-90 House" for all of its triangulations, the house's multi-level floor plan was shaped by structural and climactic considerations, thus becoming one of Palm Beach's first eco-friendly "green" houses.

The house was set on the southerly point of Island Drive, on a southeast point lot atop a raised foundation. It was configured for large-scale entertaining with extended terraces and balconies. Protected from the rain by wide roof overhangs, a wall of Persiana louvered doors opened to the prevailing breeze and morning light. Toward the street, horizontal bands of high windows captured the afternoon sun.

House Beautiful magazine showcased the house as a 1957 Pacesetter House of the Year. Like many of Island Drive's once fashionable mid-century houses, the Mass house was demolished.

An island chain of memories

Residents recollect Everglades Island's calm tranquility as if it was located on some distant foreign shore rather than five minutes from Worth Avenue.

"Everglades Island was where my parents bought their first house when they moved to Palm Beach more than forty years ago," recalled Clare O'Keeffe. "It was a simpler, more relaxing time. The lovely sunsets across the Intracoastal veranda were an event, very peaceful and private. Living on an island off an island was safe, secluded and serene," she added.

It took another resident only a few minutes to decide that a house with lake views to the south and golf course fairways to the north would be her home for the next forty-five years.

Jane Will Smith lives on one of Island Road's oldest houses. Designed in 1942 by Maurice Fatio, the house was built in the avant-garde Streamline Moderne style for Detroit industrialist Theodore Buhl and his wife, Anastasia Ziegfeld Buhl. Mrs. Buhl was showman Flo Ziegfeld's sister. Mrs. Smith, ninety-one, remembers the day she first saw the house in 1964.

"I'd heard Mrs. Wilkinson wanted to sell. My agent, Alex Obolensky, told me I wasn't going to like it. He sat in the car and smoked. I walked in; I walked back out and told him to get me this house right now. He couldn't believe it. I've been here ever since. I knew then it was my house," said Mrs. Smith.

(Left) Top: Plat map, Everglades Island.

Mrs. Smith's daughter, Jayne Teagle Keith, grew up at the Island Road house; later, buying a house for her family near on the south end of Everglades Island just over the bridge from her mother's house.

"We would fish in the ponds on the golf course, catch frogs and tadpoles; later, my sister caught barracuda in them. I suppose everything has gotten bigger in Palm Beach," recalled Mrs. Keith. "Everglades Island has always been really special; the foxes help keep the island touch."

And yet, however golden its days past, the island has undergone noticeable changes during the recent building binge that some residents believe clouds the island's future.

In the wake of the Boom

On a recent Friday afternoon, nearly fifty construction service trucks were parked on the north end of Island Drive, either off-street within several construction sites or along the street. Workmen lounged on the curbs on both sides of the streets. On another day, there were fewer than ten commercial vehicles at the same sites and none of them were parked on the street. Thus, as much as residents are perturbed about the volume of construction, it may also be the unpredictability of the street's navigability that they say seriously affects the quality of life.

One resident, who passes through the north end of Island Drive every day, expresses concern about the intensity of development.

"My husband built our house in 1956 and I have lived here for more than thirty years," said Kamila Remington, who now describes her once private and quiet location as, "a madhouse with all the building going on."

"The Town Council has established guidelines as to construction sites on a residential street and the parking of trucks," remarked John Page, the Town's director of planning, zoning and building department.

According to the Town's ordinances, each construction site may apply to public works for up to three allotted on-street parking permits for commercial vehicles. These windshield permits apply only to the use of existing legal parking spaces. There are no limits to the number of vehicles that can be parked within a residential construction site.

Since 1990, more than forty percent of Everglades Island's houses have been demolished, according to the town's building department. Most were single-story, less than five thousand-square-feet houses, replaced predominately with two-story houses built about forty- to sixty-percent larger, often with walls and gates. While some residents moved to the island to downsize, they now find themselves hedged in among more massive houses, ones they thought they had eluded when moving to Everglades Island.

"As much as I love the island, it isn't what I expected," said one resident. The ongoing construction may be going on for another several years. We should have a reasonable expectation of peace and quiet."

"I object to the island, my home, becoming a job site. There must be more Carrera marble here than in Carrera," observed one resident. "These formulaic houses take away from the island's charm. Why is it the first thing people think they have to do when they move to Palm Beach is demolish a house and build a living mausoleum to themselves? And, we have quite a few now on the island."

At a recent ARCOM meeting, commissioners approved another Venetian-style house on Island Drive, even though, according to the recorded minutes, they commented that the style may not be appropriate for Everglades Island and that building lots are maxed out. One ARCOM commissioner suggested planting a tree to mitigate the "McMansion feel of the house."

But these distractions, found today in almost every area of Palm Beach and South Florida, may not be enough to outweigh the island's market appeal. During the past four years, Island Drive properties, teardowns and new-builds, have sold from $6 million to $15 million. Current listings are priced from $11 million to $17 million.

"Everglades Island will always be desirable because it is a choice location for those who want manageable, waterfront properties," said Paulette Koch, a sales associate with The Corcoran Group.

Whether on Worth Avenue, at Town Hall or along Royal Poinciana Way, change is the essence of today's Palm Beach. The island's once smaller mid-century footprint has all but washed away, leaving some residents adrift with a sense of dislocation rather than appreciating the developing diversity. Everglades Island was never formatted as a context for a stucco-and-barrel tile skyline with ornamental showplaces framed by tall thick ficus hedges and gates.

And yet, this island on an island retains its irresistible charms. Island Road's stately row of royal palms frame picturesque views of the Everglades Club fairways, ponds and greens. The island's tropical vegetation, the southeast ocean breezes, and the waterway and lagoon that encircle it are relatively unchanged. More than seventy years later, Everglades Island remains Palm Beach's most desirable secluded treasure.

(Right) Top: On Everglades Island, post-World War II modern houses were built in the more intimate villa style. *(Palm Beach Daily News)*

Bottom: Tarpon Island. A gated bridge leads to Tarpon Island, the only private residential island in Palm Beach.

Palm Beach Regency

Palm Beach architecture's uncommon mix of artifice and authenticity transforms the island's houses into incomparable showplaces, none more eclectic, fantastic and unexpected than those inspired and fashioned from early 19th-century Regency architecture.

Unlike the Mediterranean and Caribbean styles that are rooted to the island's history, location and climate, Palm Beach's posh Regency style is widely-considered an interpretation of England's stately Late Georgian aristocratic facades. For example, unlike the 1920's Mediterranean Revival style that reproduced actual facsimiles of classical orders, Doric, Ionic and Corinthian columns, Palm Beach's artful Regency style fabricated history by implementing geometric capitals and columns molded without regard for any recognizable historical precedent.

Palm Beach's Regency style is most often illustrated by architect John Volk's designs for the Royal Poinciana Plaza and Royal Poinciana Playhouse, designer-builder Clarence Mack's houses, and developer Robert Gottfried's stately formal compositions, as designed by architect John B. Gosman.

Despite the number of Palm Beach houses characterized as Regency, when the Landmarks Preservation Commission recommended that the Palm Beach Town Council designate the Royal

(Left) Top Left: The Royal Poinciana Plaza's commercial shopping center design was an adaptation of the English Regency style.

(Left) Top Right: Regents Park, entrance feature. This late 1950s subdivision is located south of the Mar-a-Lago Club.

(Left) Bottom: 500 Regents Park Road is the centerpiece of builder Clarence Mack's South End subdivision inspired by architect John Volk's Royal Poinciana Plaza.

Poinciana Plaza and Playhouse as local landmarks, it probably never realized the Town had never historically designated a property as significant for its post-World War II Regency style.

"After a review of the local register of landmarks and a re-look at the Florida Master Site File for all our landmarks, none are listed as Regency," said Jane Day, the town's historic preservation consultant.

And further emphasizing the plaza and playhouse's unprecedented standing, according to state and national architectural scholars, a 20th century Regency-styled building has never been historically designated in either Florida or the United States.

Regency rules

"I have never seen the term Regency used in regard to post-World War II architecture, or even pre-war architecture in Florida, that would ordinarily be labeled as Neoclassical Revival," said William Carl Shriver Ph.D., registrar for the National Register of Historic Places at Florida's Bureau of Historic Preservation.

"I know that I have never used the term in regard to buildings in Florida and do not think it is one of the classifications used by the Florida Master Site File."

Properties are designated historic by state and national organizations according to the integrity of their design and the period in which they were created.

According to the National Trust's documentation guidelines, the Regency style refers only to Early Republic properties built between 1780 and 1830, a transitional movement between the Georgian and Victorian era that approximates the term of the Prince Regent under George III and, following his father's death, his reign as George IV. Hence, Savannah and Charleston's early 19th-century Regency buildings are historically-designated as Regency.

While the National Trust acknowledges Neoclassical Revival as an early 20th-century design, it cites only the following post-war design styles as historic — International, Wrightian, Brutalism, California or Ranch, Modern and Deco Moderne. As a result, Regency is not a viable post-war design classification suitable for nomination to the National Register on the basis of its architectural design.

"You are in some uncharted terrain in the 1950s and beyond. This 1950's interpretation of Regency style was explored in the design of private residences and interiors in both Palm Beach as well as Beverly Hills. It is mostly a post-World War II phenomenon." said Jeff Burden, Ph.D., architectural historian for the National Trust.

A consultant for the Center of Antique Architecture, Paris, and the Villa Medici, Rome, Dr. Burden is an architect and an archaeologist, the only American architect to have been a Fellow at the American School of Classical Studies, the American Academy, Rome, and the Ecole des Beaux-Arts, Paris.

"What you see in these Palm Beach residences was an interest in the slim elegance of English Regency style of the early-19th century. To date, it is a somewhat less touched upon area of scholarship," said Burden.

And yet, the Landmarks Preservation Commission's designation report makes numerous references to the plaza and the playhouse as examples of Regency architecture.

Previously, in 2006, ARCOM unanimously accepted a demolition report for a Clarence Mack built Regency-style house on South County Road, finding the property "without any historical or redeeming architectural features to justify preserving the residence."

And further, ARCOM explains the style as follows: "The so-called Regency style of Palm Beach has come to mean a one-story, symmetrical flat-roofed structure with classical ornamentation, stucco banding, keystones, window surrounds, arched windows, pediments, columns, elongated windows…"

This generic description does little to associate the building type with England's Regency style between c.1780-1830, a period of powdered wigs, top hats and period costumes when Late Georgian-era designers formulated a picturesque aesthetic hybrid from an assortment of classical styles, most often traced from Grand Tour sketchbooks and inspired by the ruins at Herculaneum and Pompeii. The Georgian royal court was renowned for masques, banquets and pageants, a style of excess more closely related to the earlier French Directoire and Empire style found during the Regency of Louis XV than Palladio's more functional and symmetrical Roman style imported a century earlier by architect Inigo Jones.

When British Regency architects were not designing a palace or gilding a hall, their best-known architectural form was expressed in multi-story townhouse developments like London's Regent Park. Other examples are Montpelier Crescent and Brighton's Norfolk Square or Western Terrace, all adorned with enriched pediments, elaborate pilasters, ironwork balconies and verandas.

Nearly one hundred thirty years later, Palm Beach created its own adaptation of the aristocratic Regency style. Whether it was the Phipps family's appreciation for English culture, the Duke and Duchess of Windsor-effect, or the architect's preference to blend "trend and tradition," as expressed in the designation report, the Royal Poinciana Plaza and the Royal Poinciana Playhouse were designed as if they were a tableau vivant found in Jane Austen's novel, *Sense and Sensibility*.

Clarence Mack's Tropical Empire

As the plaza and playhouse neared completion, Midwest builder-developer Clarence Mack planned Regent Park, a subdivision of five houses placed around a circular drive that framed a central open park in the South End, designed in a residential style closely akin to Volk's commercial Royal Poinciana Plaza.

But, as much as the two projects appear analogous, there was a critical difference: John Volk was an architect, whose expertise was his tailored design for clients. Clarence Mack was not an architect but a designer-builder known for his mass appeal. Mack was a former window dresser who two decades earlier had moved to Palm Beach from Cleveland, Ohio, where he was a spec builder packaging turn-key houses for the family's construction business.

Previously, between 1914 and 1938, Mack design-built more than thirty houses in Lakewood and Shaker Heights, Ohio, converting pattern-book exteriors into mansions for newly-minted millionaires who wanted an old-money look. He interchanged various façades and doorways, detailing and altering them with his own palette of French eclectic and Georgian features.

(Right) Top: In Parc Monceau, rooflines are trimmed with urns and statuary.

(Right) Bottom Left: Parc Monceau. Built by Clarence Mack following Regents Park, Parc Monceau is south of Widener's Curve on the Ocean Boulevard.

(Right) Bottom Right: This North End façade's Regency-style features composite columns not based on any classical order.

"Though everyone still calls him an architect, I have never seen any evidence that Clarence Mack studied architecture, apprenticed as an architect or was ever actually a licensed architect in Ohio or Florida," said Ann Marie Wieland, archivist for the Cleveland Public Library, the repository for the Clarence Mack archives.

Mack's father and grandfather were builders. Having learned the trade from them, he served as his own designer and contractor, usually living in each of the houses before he sold them. He installed crystal chandeliers, Chippendale mirrors, marble mantels, planted English-style gardens, filled rooms with French and English antiques, and added powder rooms and libraries where he leather-tooled the bookends to match the woodwork.

"He had a wonderful eye and was self-taught working in the family's building business," Wieland added, whose master's thesis included a survey of Clarence Mack's work.

Mack's early Palm Beach houses were modeled on his 1920's Ohio houses, making slight modifications and accessorizing the façades with urns and statues. Before he platted Regent Park, he had built Neoclassical Revival-style houses, which he called Tropical Empire, on Via del Lago, Jungle Road and El Vedado. Mack furnished 320 El Vedado, the home of Benson Ford. He used figurines and sconces, including Wheeler Williams sculptures. Across the street, at 319 El Vedado, he added Ionic pilasters and a lower-level garage to a near-identical façade he had used for his popular Lakewood House in Ohio.

Following the success of Regent Park, Mack developed Parc Monceau, named for a late 18th-century English-styled park in Paris. For this South Ocean Boulevard subdivision, he divided an estate-sized parcel and built seven houses formulated with the same strict geometry and decor as Regent Park.

Later, Clarence Mack's achievements attracted builder Robert Gottfried. When Gottfried arrived in Palm Beach to work in his family's construction business, he asked Mack's advice on what he should build in Palm Beach. Mack told Gottfried to specialize in one particular style and make it his own.

(Right): At 400 Regents Park Road, builder Clarence Mack designed his own waterfront house.

250

Gottfried paid Mack the highest compliment by emulating Mack's style, synthesizing less decorous exteriors with more modern, spacious interiors. Within several years, Robert Gottfried's name became synonymous with the island's most popular style, Gottfried Regency.

Gottfried Regency

Beginning with a single house on Wells Road during the 1950s, Robert Gottfried built his signature style, in partnership with architect John B. Gosman, into a definitive Palm Beach genre. Gottfried's companies controlled almost every aspect of the house's construction, having established Palm Beach Marble & Tile, Classic Moulders, Imports Unlimited, Classic Polyroof Company and the PaverLock Driveway Company.

Gottfried Regency, as *TIME* called it in 1981, became tantamount with the sophisticated luxury new Palm Beach residents expected if they didn't want to live in barrel-tiled, antiquated, oversized mansions with creaky wooden floors or multi-unit condominiums.

Gottfried's symmetrical formal facades were detailed with composites and framed by sculpted hedges, conveying a sense of restrained classicism. Beyond the double-door entrances, Gottfried introduced impressive marble-floored reception halls, Sherle Wagner bathrooms, St. Charles kitchens, silver closets, built-in security systems and oversized galleries.

In the North End, Polmer Park, Via Linda, Chateaux Drive and North Lake Way became settings for the Gottfried brand. Along Via Los Incas, Gottfried built ten mansionettes designed to look as if they had been there forever, a style he called French Gottfried, their striking similarities evocative of Mansart's Hall of Mirrors.

The architectural visions of Volk, Mack and Gottfried were uniquely Palm Beach; their Regency-style work reflects the island's unrestrained delight in mingling reality and fantasy.

(Left) Top: An impressive Gottfried Regency entrance.

(Left) Bottom: 10 Via Los Incas. With a distinctive marble balustrade, the house is often described as "Gottfried Regency."

Is it a Mizner?

For years, Palm Beach residents were exceptionally proud when they were able to declare their house or building was designed by Addison Mizner. But, as Mizner's contributions were joined by praise for other prominent architects, such as Marion Sims Wyeth and Maurice Fatio, residents often selected them for substantial alterations and additions, which in many cases were made after every season. And with many of Mizner's significant original works demolished before the Landmarks Preservation Commission (LPC) was organized in 1979, the question, "Is it a Mizner?" becomes sometimes difficult to clearly answer.

For instance, the highly-visible Moorish-styled garden arch located at 365 North County Road is regarded as one of Palm Beach's most iconic architectural symbols. In 1980, the town's LPC designated it a local landmark along with a nearby fountain. The commission officially affirmed that these were components of Addison Mizner's original design for El Mirasol, the E. T. Stotesbury's oceanfront estate known as the architect's first residential Palm Beach design.

A Mizner Mirage

But, could the arch and the fountain really be Addison Mizner's work even if they bear no resemblance to any of Mizner's known work in Palm Beach? And, if it was a Mizner, shouldn't the arch aesthetically relate to the arch Mizner designed for El Mirasol's original entrance along Ocean Boulevard?

(Left): The El Mirasol archway on North County Road remains the work of Treanor and Fatio, as documented by several illustrated articles at the time, even though it was incorrectly designated the work of Addison Mizner by the Landmarks Preservation Commission.

"I've always wondered about that," said the late architectural historian Donald W. Curl, the area's best-known Mizner scholar and author of *Mizner's Florida*. "I think the arch and fountain are most possibly Maurice Fatio's work."

Furthermore, the existing structure cannot be found in form or facsimile among the extensive collection of Mizner's architectural drawings at the Historical Society of Palm Beach County. Also, there is no trace of the arch among the architect's scrapbooks and rare book collection at The Society of Four Arts Library.

Then, if North County Road did not become the estate's primary entrance until sometime after 1929 when Ocean Boulevard was washed out during the hurricane, and permanently closed from Wells Road to the Beach Club, wouldn't that make the existent prominent feature highly unlikely?

And, most puzzling, how could these architectural follies be designated Addison Mizner's when the fountain is included as a commission of Maurice Fatio's in a book on Treanor & Fatio's work?

"My father lost quite a few plans and records during the hurricanes and I would not be surprised if it is my father's work," said Alexandra Fatio Taylor, author of the book on her father's Palm Beach houses. "Palm Beach architects often worked on each other's houses."

She opened her book, *Maurice Fatio*, and pointed to page 208.

"Clearly, the fountain designated a Mizner is a Fatio work. Also, the arch looks quite similar to my father's work," Taylor said.

According to Town Hall records, the venerable preservationist Barbara Hoffstott, wrote Landmarks Chairman, Robert Grace, a letter in January 1980 expressing concern that there was no research or documentation verifying the arch and the fountain as Mizner's. She wrote, " … to document these will be expensive … My inclination is to be frugal with taxpayer's money…" Thus, Hoffstott encouraged the commission to move forward and designate the fountain and garden arch, in fear these significant architectural artifacts might be demolished before the designation.

In describing the distinctive portal during the May 1980 designation hearings, Landmarks Commissioner Judge James R Knott declared, "…where a structure was so well known locally as to be common knowledge, documentation was not necessary … since the gate was so famous and we all know its background and history, that it was unnecessary to document it as the advent of Mizner's career as an architect in this area and considered by many citizens as a monument in the community."

Town Attorney Skip Randolph advised the Town Council that members "… could properly designate the gate a landmark based on their own knowledge."

As a result, the Town of Palm Beach designated a landmark that twenty-eight years later is clearly credited to the wrong architect.

"Like other resorts, at the end of every season Palm Beach residents made changes to their houses," remarked Jane Day, the Town of Palm Beach's historic preservation consultant.

"In the early days the town did not have a staff to thoroughly research designations but now we are able to do more in-depth documentation. During the summer we will be updating our files and this will be one we will take a look at," Day added.

Among the Historical Society of Palm Beach County's archives, the only authentically early photo of El Mirasol's North County Road entrance is a Xerox that does not show the distinctive designated arch. Instead, it shows the existence of a small ordinary garden gate similar to the structure that now can be seen below the existing designated arch.

"When Fatio did work at another architect's house he often did not take credit for it," Donald Curl added.

Whether one owns a Mizner or a Fatio, or both, may not make a difference to some but architectural provenance is essential in giving each Palm Beach property its unique and extraordinary aura.

"This is a reminder of the importance of keeping accurate records," Day said.

Unforgettable Palm Beach

"We were so young and gay then and we thought we had all the money in the world. It will be sad if the great houses vanish and the Mizner period becomes only a memory and part of Palm Beach's past rather than its present."
— Billie Burke

Despite the heart-felt sentiment, many of Palm Beach's original showplaces and architectural masterpieces have vanished. And though Billie Burke may not be someone you readily associate with today's Palm Beach history, for many years Glinda, the Good Witch of Oz, and her husband, impresario Florenz Ziegfeld, along with their friends, the E. F. Huttons, the Gurnee Munns and the Harrison Williamses, were members of the resort's leading Café Society set, at home at the B&T as well as at the Stork Club.

Thirty years later, Miss Burke starred in several Palm Beach Playhouse productions, often staying with her close friend Marjorie Post at Mar-a-Lago. It was then, during the late 1950s, she reflected on the immeasurable loss of El Mirasol and Playa Riente, later joined by the razing of Casa Florencia, La Fontana, and Casa Bendita, among others designed by architects Fatio & Treanor and Marion Sims Wyeth.

(Left) Top: Whitehall. *(Library of Congress)*

(Left) Bottom: The Banyans, South Lake Trail. The Brelsford House was demolished shortly after it was listed in the National Register of Historic Places. *(Library of Congress)*

While no longer a part of picturesque Ocean Boulevard, these lost houses exist largely within the Historical Society of Palm Beach County's collections of photographs, postcards and architectural drawings housed in vertical files and Hollinger boxes. More often, Palm Beach's most notable places are remembered for the circumstances surrounding their downfall rather than the splendor of their heyday.

For years after a significant building has been eliminated from the town's historic framework, if not by accident then either by whim or the need to be modern, stories and photographs recap the unfolding melodrama from showplace to scrap heap or the spectacle of ruin. And when considering this ever-shifting kaleidoscope of architectural styles and trends, you must remember the resort's history is uniquely episodic. For many years, the newspaper was never published between April and November. Thus, it is a narrative recorded within a series of seasonal cycles shaded by each era's perspectives, yet guided by the primary principle that by virtue of living in Palm Beach is to be unconstrained by rules or boundaries.

There are numerous illustrations of this deeply-rooted pattern that has always been an inherent aspect of Palm Beach's accustomed charm. Whether the baffling drawing-room mystery resulting from the demolition of Blythedunes, the puzzling inquisition into the Four Winds' demolition and reconstruction, or on a far more operatic scale, L'Encantada's cursed tugboat ride to oblivion, Palm Beach's flair for denouements can never be understated, especially when paradox is the prevailing rationale.

Palm Beach houses are the quintessential barometer for measuring the island's prominence and significance just as its grand hotels once defined it as a fashionable international winter resort. Although now regarded by their price and size, these villas, castles, and mansions are usually the key components for recounting the town's history. Subjects of unceasing fascination, the design and construction of opulent lavish houses — their owners, architects, and craftsmen — determines how today's Palm Beach is perceived and appreciated.

(Right) Top Left: The Royal Poinciana Hotel. *(Library of Congress)*

(Right) Top Right: Palm Beach-The Most Popular Resort in the World.

(Right) Bottom: Many of Playa Riente's priceless artifacts can be found in Vero Beach where the one and only Waldo Sexton saved many of Addison Mizner's aesthetic fixtures from houses the Town of Palm Beach permitted to be demolished.

Palm Beach Florida

Most Popular Resort in the World

Hotel Royal Poinciana
Fred Sterry and H. E. Bemis, Managers

The Breakers
Leland Sterry, Manager

Eighteen-Hole Golf Course. Deep-sea Fishing from Ocean Pier. Surf and Pool Bathing. Electric and Naptha Launches and Sail Boats on Lake Worth. Finest Trails for Bicycle Chairs in the World. A Southern Resort With Surf Bathing. Equable Sunny Climate. Superb Hotel Accommodations. Finest and Most Romantic Scenery on Earth

"EVERYBODY GOES TO PALM BEACH"

Ever since Whitehall's imposing facade and ballroom, "replete with marble, tapestries, paintings and arcades," rendered passé the island's existing porch-and-parlor cottages, Palm Beach has been captivated by the aura of spectacular showplaces. And significantly, Whitehall's ornate supersized presence made for Palm Beach's first trophy house. Designed by Carrere and Hastings, Whitehall became a standard, influencing others compelled to build the ultimate mansion. The architects designed Whitehall in between two of their most prominent public buildings — the Library of Congress interiors and the House and Senate Office Buildings. However more apropos on Bellevue Avenue or Fifth Avenue, Whitehall's eclectic adaptive mix of styles, part European palace, part Gilded Age country house with a southern tropical adaptation, also served as a model for Palm Beach's predilection for synthetic architectural styles. Although it still stands in the

middle of Palm Beach, Whitehall is no longer the centerpiece for the resort world that created it. And yet, its seminal influence in redefining the Palm Beach standard can never be understated.

Today's Palm Beach is not so much a resort destination as it is a private residential enclave dominated by the real estate industry where houses, not hotels, are the iconic symbol of arrival and accomplishment. People build oversized chateaus and palazzos in Palm Beach that might be judged ostentatious in their home towns. Unfortunately, the history of architecture, as well as the

Top: Duck's Nest, North Lake Way.

historic preservation movement, regularly focuses on private palaces like Whitehall and larger-than-life public places rather than everyday landmarks that contribute to a shared community experience, such as the houses that once defined Palm Beach's Midtown and North End. These humble undesignated houses are routinely scrapped, no matter how rich in historic lore, reminders of a time when human scale was the primary criterion rather than the exception.

Interestingly, when the town's Landmarks Preservation Commission was established in 1980, commissioners judged anomalous many of the homes built by the pioneer families, considered by some as Palm Beach's authentic lakeside cottages that were dwarfed by Whitehall's presence. In so many words, one councilman destined them for oblivion when he said, "This is Palm Beach, these aren't houses people associate with Palm Beach; they belong on Boston's North Shore."

While Duck's Nest remains along North Lake Way, through the mindful diligence of the Maddock family who still own it, The Banyans, Dulciora, Fleur D' Eau, and Primavera were demolished. The Cluett family's Bywater Lodge was also destroyed. When Joseph Riter bought the Cluett's North Lake Way cottage in 1916, he renamed it Al Poniente and retained Vizcaya's architect F. Burrall Hoffman to design Palm Beach's first large-scale home entertainment center. The thirty-five-by-seventy-feet lakeside room was decorated in the Renaissance style with a cypress ceiling painted by the same artist who had enhanced Vizcaya's grotto pool. This setting for daily afternoon musicales and tableau vivant productions was said to inspire the founding of The Society of the Four Arts.

The era's pre-mansion cottages were valued for something more priceless than their architecture; they gave Palm Beach an irreplaceable sense of place. Reve d'Ete in the North End and Figulus in the South End were both landmarks consigned to the wrecking ball. Before visitors ever thought of coming to Palm Beach to buy houses, they came to wander around an island jungle, wonder at its gardens, and be photographed standing next to its magnificent trees.

At their Garden of Eden, as Charles and Frances Cragin called Reve d'Ete, the couple imported hundreds of exotic species they discovered during their worldwide travels. To the south

(Right) Top: Although the memory of the second Breakers has faded, destroyed by fire and replaced by Shultze and Weaver's more European-style hotel, it was considered one of the grand seaside resorts. *(Library of Congress)*

(Right) Bottom: The Maddock family's Palm Beach Hotel was destroyed by the catastrophic Breakers fire. *(Library of Congress)*

at Figulus, Charles and Mary Bingham entrusted Dr. David Fairchild to supervise the plantings, also introducing new species on the island.

But Whitehall's enormity would not stand alone forever amidst the cottage colony. By World War I, Henry Phipps, the former Pittsburgh partner of Andrew Carnegie who retired when the Carnegie Company was sold to J. P. Morgan, was already a considerable real estate presence, buying much of the land along Ocean Boulevard from Palm Beach to Miami. Eventually, the Phipps family owned most of Palm Beach.

In 1914, Phipps had purchased ocean-to-lake parcels along Palm Beach's newly surveyed and built North Ocean Boulevard. Here the Phipps family built Villa Artemis and Heamaw, the first large-scale oceanfront mansions that after the war began the trend that transformed Palm Beach into a residential community in the style of Newport and Bar Harbor. The Phippses selected F. Burrall Hoffman as their architect who at the time was working on Vizcaya, the James Deering mansion in Miami.

Like Vizcaya and Whitehall, Villa Artemis and Heamaw were centered on large interior patios. Also, both houses had side entrances and columned loggias on the first and second floor overlooking the pool. In addition, the Phipps family added a house by an unknown architect to the south for Mr. Phipps' father-in-law Michael Grace. Later, it underwent a complete renovation by architect Marion Sims Wyeth and became known as Las Incas.

While the style of the Phipps houses followed the more grandiose formality established by Whitehall, after World War I something happened on Palm Beach's way to copying the white wedding-cake mansion styles dictated by Beaux-Arts New York and Philadelphia architects. When the influential Stotesburys switched from a Horace Trumbauer design to Addison Mizner's for El Mirasol, it forever changed the island's architectural profile An eclectic California-inspired architect, Addison Mizner, introduced a less formal Spanish style, giving Palm Beach a picturesque skyline. "I begin with monasteries and convents and end up with palaces," said Mizner in his unpublished autobiography.

Spanish and Italian styles sprang up all over Palm Beach as more casual Hispano-Moorish styles in Midtown contrasted with formal houses in the North End and South End Mansion District, rendered in the Italian Renaissance vernacular. Then, almost as quickly as it began, the 1920s boom busted due to a confluence of factors — hurricanes, economy, and changes in taste and style.

The previous generation's great houses were demolished.

From the 1930s to 1980, Palm Beachers embraced Modernism. Despite decades of popularity synonymous with the best Modernist design in the world, during the past twenty-five years Palm Beach has retreated into the artifice of contextual historical facades rather than embrace artful contemporary designs. With the advent of its Landmarks Commission, the town reinvented itself as "a Mediterranean-style Mecca of architectural beauty."

Today's mammoth houses are built on the order of resorts and office buildings. During the past decade the average house size has dramatically increased. A new generation of colossal houses was hatched — full-sized estates crowded onto compact suburban lots. These houses reflect the obsession with building to the limits rather than conserving space and maintaining architectural integrity. Although local zoning laws were established to protect property owners from transgressions on their neighbor's quality of life, many building codes were based on minimum square-foot requirements without distinct maximum constraints, leading to the town's current shifting ground where simply big houses are being built.

Since 1980, square footage has been one of the key elements in determining the greatness of houses. Size is emphasized rather than scale, and house designs are packaged for their potential to frame high volume interiors. During the past twenty-five years, more than five hundred single family houses have been leveled with more than three hundred demolitions in the past decade alone. One hundred of these have been fifty years and older, though deemed unworthy of landmark designation. Thus, while Palm Beach has lost many of its character-defining houses that created its fabric, it may have amassed the largest collection of super-sized houses in the United States.

Palm Beach was built as a resort, a place to escape the world, not reflect it. And yet, everywhere you look in Palm Beach you see construction. As you drive around the island, there are an ever growing number of spec houses with spec designs. Facades and floor plans are designed to sell rather than on any aesthetic. Can houses designed to sell ever be great houses? Is greatness determined by the number of features in the home entertainment system or the size of a wine cellar? Is it all these things or is it the thing we cannot express, that makes a house incomparable, unique, and unparalleled? Is it the people who once lived in it or the ones who designed it?

Sometimes, it might be beneficial to recall past achievements however much they might be overshadowed by today's even greater realization. Certainly, Schultze and Weaver's magnificent

266

design for The Breakers has ensured its timeless presence. Yet, memories of The Breakers built in 1904, known as the Florida East Coast Hotel Company's "most elegant hotel," have nearly vanished as anecdotes and images of the fire that destroyed it in March 1925 are repeated so frequently.

Described as much like the casino in Newport, Breakers II was built during the height of the Gilded Age, following a fire that leveled the hotel's original structure. More than a thousand craftsmen worked in two shifts for six months so that the Duchess of Sutherland could be among the first guests to register in February 1904. A forty-piece orchestra played daily at noon on the verandah with more elaborate concerts staged on the oceanfront grand piazza.

The new Breakers was designed to be the most colorful of all Henry Flagler's network of hotels. The central lobby, painted in green and old ivory, looked west across the golf course to the Royal Poinciana Hotel and east onto verandahs with ocean panoramas. The flanking card rooms were painted yellow. Each of the four hundred and thirty-two rooms was equipped with a telephone, radiator, and cherry-wood furnishings with brass-mounted white-iron beds. While there were forty three-room suites with two baths, for the first time every room featured two entrances, thus guests and their servants were given the possibility of a limitless number of connected rooms.

The main dining room was red and white with burlap wall coverings. The dining room's capacity of slightly-more than six hundred consisted of one hundred and thirty-eight four- and six-person tables. The banquet hall was rendered in browns while the casual Art Nouveau café was furnished with Mission-style tables and chairs.

But then, at the end of the 1925 season, much like its predecessor, this vivid seaside folly burned to the ground, giving rise to a more foreign Mediterranean vision rather than one more closely akin to the Bar Harbor and Long Island summer seasons that once characterized the familiarity of a Palm Beach winter.

Rather than by an accidental fire, Playa Riente's demise was probably due to spite. The lasting impressions of Playa Riente's architectural grandeur and unrivaled craftsmanship, considered

(Left) Top: Although a significant landmark in the history of resort Palm Beach, The Breakers golf cottage on Cocoanut Row was never designated and was demolished.

(Left) Bottom: The demolition of the picturesque cottage colony at The Breakers made way for condominiums.

among Palm Beach's greatest houses, have all but been replaced by owner Anna Dodge's prolonged legal scuffles. While it seems unlikely that Dodge's fortune was ever as pinched as she claimed, her run-ins with her neighbors prompted her to settle the matter with the town by destroying Playa Riente, as well as not missing a chance for a chic garage sale, auction, and dinner dance at the same time.

Built in 1923 for oilman Joshua Cosden, Playa Riente expressed the vast unconstrained grandeur most often associated with Palm Beach. Along with a myriad of loggias, cloisters, sun decks, patios, and terraces, there was a cathedral-like living room and a music room, not only made famous by its performers and guests but its museum-quality nine-panel mural painted by Jose Sert.

Acquired by Anna Dodge in 1926, Playa Riente's mammoth scale and extent rivaled European palaces. Three weeks after Dodge bought Addison Mizner's magnificent seventy-room showplace set on twenty-seven ocean-to-lake acres, she married her much-younger real estate agent, former actor Hugh Dillman. Playa Riente became as well known for its patios as its parties, featuring fifteen master bedrooms and a bachelor's wing permitting single male guests to come and go without being announced.

Twenty years later, the May-December marriage soured as did Palm Beach's mansion market. The widow-divorcee found no one who would fork over one-quarter of the $4 million she had paid in the mid-1920s. Anna Dodge spent years attempting to rezone the house as a museum, school or private club. Although located adjacent to the Palm Beach Country Club, her neighbors complained. "Big houses are a drag on the market, nobody wants to live in Playa Riente …" wrote *Palm Beach Post* writer Helen Van Hoy Smith. 'Upkeep and taxes were a headache," Dodge was quoted as saying. She hosted a series of final parties and a three-day "everything-must-go" sale. Then, she demolished the house in 1957.

Several years later, when Big Chief Wrecking Company pulled a permit in January 1961 to demolish Casa Bendita, it was not a surprise when the new owner said, "Great old palaces are no longer attractive to modern buyers. The demand now is for less pretentious but strictly modern dwellings." Casa Bendita, once an exemplar for the town's finest architecture, became an illustration for "Palm Beach's flamboyant history," wrote one newspaper. Often called Phipps Castle because of its elaborate entrance highlighted by a four-story octagonal tower, Casa Bendita was built by John S. Phipps on the highest point of the ridgeline along three hundred and seventy-five feet of oceanfront when Ocean Boulevard still extended in front of houses from Wells Road to the Palm Beach Country Club. With principal rooms facing the ocean, an open staircase led to the second floor's eight master bedrooms. Its dining room was covered in Venetian red brocades, and Casa Bendita was the setting for some of Palm Beach's most notable social events. No matter, Casa Bendita became a street name for a subdivision.

Unlike the fate that befell Playa Riente and Casa Bendita, in 1947 Cielito Lindo's owner was able to save the main house by slicing it into several houses separated by Kings Road, as news reports of that period framed the story. The existing structures can only hint at its former grandeur. Designed by Marion Sims Wyeth for James and Jessie Donahue in 1927 and situated north of Mar-a-Lago, Cielito Lindo was one of Palm Beach's most magnificent ocean-to-lake estates.

"Dulce est desipere in loco" remains inscribed on Cielito Lindo's garden wall as an epitaph from the 1920's era of excess. The Latin quote from Horace's Odes translates to, "It is good to play the fool at times." Among Palm Beach's most fabled escapist landscapes, Cielito Lindo's turquoise and emerald plantings were reportedly selected as they favored the Atlantic Ocean's colorful palette. Unconstrained by reason or means, and though never regarded as avid gardeners, the Donahues amassed a breathtaking supernatural display of purple bougainvillea hedges, beds of ageratum edged with pink begonias, heavenly hibiscus, tropical wisteria, and Xanadu philodendron. Gardenias were abloom like white caps magically transformed at night by torches and fireflies into a sublime surreal illusion.

Although James and Jessie May Woolworth Donahue never entertained on the scale of their Mar-a-Lago neighbors E.F. and Marjorie Hutton, who staged full-length plays and welcomed the Ringling Brothers Circus, they would regale their guests with an occasional after-dinner baritone.

When the end came for El Mirasol, there were few who could recall the house's significant role in the town's architectural and social history. The one hundred and forty-seven-room oceanfront house happened to be architect Addison Mizner's first Palm Beach residential commission. A year after Eva Stotesbury died, auctioneers announced an "everything must go" sale. More than four thousand attended the weekend affair where guests became registered bidders after paying a $2 admission fee. A decade later, El Mirasol was demolished in 1958.

For Blythedunes, the end was less anticipated. "If Harrison and Mona Williams made 513 North County Road into one of Palm Beach's largest mansions, Charles and Jayne Wrightsman made it one of the resort's most important," wrote the late Donald Curl. Nonetheless, however

When the end came for El Mirasol, there were few who could recall the house's significant role in the town's architectural and social history.

magnificent, it was demolished two days after Leslie Wexner bought it in 1984. At the time, much of the town expressed surprise that despite its impressive provenance and splendor, it had never been designated a local landmark.

Designed in 1917 by architect Hastings Mundy, Blythedunes was initially built for Robert Dun Douglass, whose father Benjamin Douglass and uncle Robert G. Dun founded the firm that became Dun & Bradstreet. Blythedunes remained a traditional U-shaped Tuscan-style house until Douglas sold the property to Harrison and Mona Williams in 1930. A utility magnate, Williams, one of the world's richest men, retained Treanor & Fatio to make additions to the house. They included a twenty-eight-by-thirty-foot dining room and a twenty-eight-by-fifty-foot drawing room, transforming the formal beach house into an incomparable showplace. With Mona Williams declared one of the best dressed women in the world, who else would she call in but Syrie Maugham to create the house's modernist interior décor?

After the Wrightsmans acquired the house in 1947, Jayne Wrightsman retained French decorator Stephane Boudin to convert Blythedunes into a 17th- and 18th- century French show house, complete with parquet de Versailles floors from the Palais Royal in Paris. A 1984 *House and Garden* magazine article speculated that Blythedunes, with its Metropolitan Museum of Art security system, "may well have sheltered more great works of art than any other house in the United States." Nonetheless, the house was destroyed.

Whether by importing architectural styles from distant places or recreating far-flung eras, every generation has imposed its own interpretation of what Palm Beach represents. And while Palm Beach has landmarked more than two hundred and fifty buildings, many of the town's great

Left Top Left : At Louwana, a Mizner Industries lantern continues to light an upstairs hall nearly a century after it was first installed.

Left Top Right: Villa El Sarmiento. Before numbered street addresses, Palm Beach houses were known by their name.

(Left) Middle Right: La Fontana, exterior staircase. Addison Mizner's magnificent La Fontana was demolished to make room for the 100 Royal Palm Way condominium. *(Historical Society of Palm Beach County)*

(Left) Middle Left: Blythedunes was torn down to accommodate a more formal reproduction of a French-inspired architectural genre. *(The Society of the Four Arts)*

(Left) Bottom: Bobby and Kitty Glendinning canoe in the Everglades Club basin.

houses exist only as street names and names for platted subdivisions. Yet, for the most part, it is still the lost landmarks and what remains of the town's authentic architectural treasures that make up Palm Beach's extraordinary irreplaceable character.

(Left): The remarkable gardens at Ceilito Lindo enhanced the architectural showcase. *(Historical Society of Palm Beach County)*

(Right): Boar's Head and Yule Log Festival, 2011. Courtyard, The Episcopal Church of Bethesda-by-the-Sea.

Augustus Mayhew was born in Camaguey, Cuba, where his grandfather was among the post-Spanish American War pioneers from New England. They settled La Gloria, the first American colony in Cuba. He grew up in Delray Beach and received a bachelor's degree in English Literature and History from Florida State University, having also studied at the International Study Center in Florence, Italy. Along with appointments to local, regional and state historic preservation organizations, he served as archivist and chairman of archives and collections for the Historical Society of Palm Beach County. He considers himself as much a cultural explorer as a social historian and historic preservationist. His essays and photographs appear regularly in the *Palm Beach Daily News* and *the New York Social Diary*.

www.ingramcontent.com/pod-product-compliance
Lightning Source LLC
Chambersburg PA
CBHW081158230426
43666CB00016B/2853